Enjoy!

IMAGE

WHO GOD SAYS YOU ARE

JAKE JEFFCOAT

for Madeline

|| CONTENTS ||

|| FOREWORD ||

If you're anything like me, I'm sure you've asked the question, "How do people see me?" It's easy to define who we are by what we have accomplished, who we know, and even, in some situations, the mistakes we've made. Our image is something we all hold close, often closer than we should. We want our life to be known, but only known for its victories. Our generation has the ability to be seen and to be known more than ever. Through social media and other platforms, what we eat, who we know, and what we accomplish can all be broadcasted to the entire world in a matter of seconds.

It's easy to paint a picture; it's easy to tell a story; it's easy to create what we want people to see. The very image we have always wanted is the one we paint for others to view: an image that makes others strive, an image that pulls people in, an image that is usually just a far-off version of who we wish we could be. The polished-up, buttoned-up, pretty version. The popular-friends, healthy-eating version. We just want to be seen.

When I first met Jake, right away I loved his passion for people and his authenticity. Throughout these pages Jake will challenge you to re-examine what you see and who you are. His approach challenges us to take a deeper look at not just how we view ourselves, but how we see God and how God sees us. I am so excited about the opportunity you have to hear from Jake. His honesty and passion will inspire you, challenge you, and, I believe, affirm the truths our generation desperately needs.

—Caleb Stanley
Co-founder of The Alternative

TIM'S STORY

*The following story is based on the countless
number of stories I have heard over the years.
Although this story is not explicitly true,
stories like this happen every day to young people
across the United States and the world. . . .*

The bathroom door shut behind him as he leaned over the vanity, looking at himself in the mirror. The lines in his face made him look older than he was, and the torment of high school seemed to make them worse. He splashed some water on his face, and went to lie down on his bed without bothering to towel off. As he lay there, with the clothes he had worn to school still on, all he could do was look at the ceiling fan moving around and around. Never changing direction, never doing anything different—just continually spinning. It reminded him of himself.

Tim was a 17-year-old junior in high school. He spent every day for the last three years trying to find a way to speed up time so he could graduate and be done with school already. He hadn't had any luck.

Tim came from a rough home. His dad died when he was 11, and that prompted his mom to start using drugs to cope with the pain. Tim was an only child, which added to the loneliness he felt at school. The monotony of his everyday life was almost unbearable. The bus picked him up at 7:15 every morning and he sat by himself the whole way to school. He stayed in the back of all his classes, and only spoke when spoken to. At lunch he sat at a table with a few other people who were similar to him, but they didn't talk much. They mainly just tried to finish their food without drawing too much attention to the fact that they had no friends.

Tim wasn't necessarily socially awkward, and he didn't hate people. He wanted friends; he was just shy. He wasn't the type of person who would go up to a stranger and start a conversation. And nobody ever went up to him to start one. He wasn't a victim of bullies, at least no more than the average high school junior was. He wasn't on any sports teams, and because of his friendlessness and shyness he never went to any of the games. Most of his classmates saw him as a quiet, smart student who kept to himself. But Tim saw himself as a loser. He viewed himself as unworthy and not good enough for other people to care about him. He couldn't see the intelligence that was in him because loneliness clouded his view. His self-perception was detrimental to him.

Tim would lay on his bed and look at the fan every day when he got home from school. He would usually drift off to sleep, and feel guilty about feeling sad when he woke up. His life seemed so dead to him. He was being crushed under the weight of feeling alone, useless, not good enough, and unworthy. It was all he could do to fix himself a sandwich at night for dinner. He never knew if his mom was going to come home or not, and frankly it didn't matter. Tim could never believe that his mom loved him more than she loved her drugs. After all, she would choose them over him most days.

Tim was trapped. Trapped in a cycle of feeling alone and unworthy of other people's affection. His own mom spent more time with her dealers than she did with him, and he felt like nobody at school even knew his name. He had been slowly collapsing under the weight of these depressing thoughts and feelings. He didn't see a way to escape the demons that haunted every crevasse in his mind. He felt like nobody would notice if he was gone. He felt like nobody would care.

On this particular day Tim had decided that he'd had enough. He got up from his bed with his mind made up. He was going to put an end to the pain of feeling unworthy and alone. He was going to put an end to his life.

He fumbled around his room looking for a pencil and a sheet of paper so he could leave at least one thing behind for his mom. He found some in the very bottom of his book bag. He tried to straighten out the crumpled piece of paper on the edge of the desk that was in his room. He sat there for half an hour. Writing something down, then erasing it. He felt like he didn't have anything to say. He didn't even know where to start. Finally, after starting and stopping ten different times, he just scribbled one line on the piece of paper and walked out of the bedroom.

Tim walked downstairs numb to everything but his own loneliness. "I'm worthless," he thought to himself as he grabbed his mother's car keys from the bowl on the kitchen counter. He opened the door that led to the garage and then shut it behind him. He pressed the button on the wall to close the garage door to the outside air. He took a deep breath, unlocked his mom's car, sat in the driver's seat, turned on the ignition, and never got up.

At 9:13 the next morning, Tim's mom stumbled through the front door. A friend had just dropped her off. She was in pain from a long night out, and felt bad for spending another night away from her son. She knew that it was past time for Tim to be at school, but she decided she would try to do something nice to make up for staying out all night again. So she slowly made her way up the stairs to Tim's room so she could do his laundry for him.

She was confused when she got there and his lights were on. Tim always turned his lights off when he left for school. She brushed off the confusion and started picking up his dirty clothes from the floor. That's when she noticed the sheet of crumpled paper on his desk. She squinted her eyes so she could make out what the scribbled handwriting said. Confused and disoriented, she read the words that Tim had written the night before:

I'm sorry I was never good enough.

THE PROBLEM OF A GENERATION

It was an ordinary college day when I made the realization that would lead me to write this book. It was my junior year of college and I was sitting quietly in my communications and research methods class taught by Professor Kim.

It was the third class meeting of the semester so we were really just beginning to dive into the material. Professor Kim instructed the class to break up into small groups for the project he had just assigned, a 30-page paper based on empirical research we would perform. Luckily, I had a couple of my friends in that class so I naturally drifted over to them. We formed our little group and started discussing possible topics for our paper. My friend Makayla had already written down some options for us and there was one that immediately stuck out to me.

The negative effects on self-image due to comparison through social media outlets.

That was it. I knew that's what I wanted to do our paper on. I didn't know why yet, but I voiced immediately that I was all in for that topic, and the group quickly agreed with me.

Later, our professor said that he wanted to go around the room and have each group share their chosen topic. He first called on a group across the room from us that happened to have a couple of my other friends in it. So my friend Rob stood up and proceeded to announce to the class what his group's topic was.

The negative effect on self-image due to comparison through social media outlets.

Certainly this was a joke. There was no way that they came up with the exact same topic as us. Since Rob was my friend I glared at him from across the room and mouthed to him that he had better change his topic. He didn't.

Then something incredible happened. As our professor went from group to group I caught a glimpse, for the very first time, of what my generation's biggest struggle was: self-image.

Every single group in my class had almost the same exact topic. One group stood up and said,

"Comparison and the negative effects that it brings to self-esteem." Another group said, "The effects of scandalous advertisement on the self-perception of millennials." And still another group said, "The negative effects of bullying on self-image."

At this point the entire class was almost laughing because everybody had come up with essentially the same topic for our research papers. But I wasn't. I just sat at my desk and looked around. My heart had just broken. As I looked at everybody in my class all I could think about was how each of them had been created in the image of God, and how obviously at some point they had become oblivious to that fact.

I looked over to Makayla and said to her, "Hey Makayla, what do you think the biggest problem for our generation is?" She just kind of laughed and said that was too heavy of a question for an 8:00 a.m. class. But for some reason I couldn't get that question out of my head. For the next 48 hours I asked a few dozen people what they thought the biggest problem our millennial generation struggled with was. About two-thirds of them said self-image. There were other answers too— commitment, patience, entitlement—but as soon as I brought up self-image and comparison, each person would say, "That's it. That's our biggest problem."

With determination, I started thinking about what causes this self-image problem that so many people have. I knew that comparing our physical appearance with others through social media played a big part in it, but I also knew that wasn't the only factor. I started thinking of all the ways people struggled with their self-image, and it quickly became apparent that people didn't just struggle with their outside appearance.

Many of the self-image problems people face come in the shape of unmet expectations. People don't live up to their own or others' expectations of them, and in turn they begin to view themselves as a failure. These problems also show up in the form of regret. So many people live in the shadow of their past mistakes, which can cause them to see themselves as unworthy. Some of these problems come in the form of academic performance. People are extremely, extremely smart, so they put all of their time into doing well in school. The moment they make one bad grade they are torn from head to toe with shame.

At the core of all of these self-image issues is an identity issue that feeds all of the anxiety we feel about life. Let me explain what I mean. Those who experience self-image problems through unmet expectations identify themselves as failures. People who live in the shadow of their past mistakes identify themselves as unworthy. People who fear academic failure are crushed when their identity as intelligent is challenged. This self-image crisis is, at its core, an identity problem because we have all failed to realize who we are. We constantly define ourselves by the wrong things, and they end up feeding the very self-image problem we hope they can destroy. We put all of our identity into earthly variables that will leave us feeling broken and empty.

So what is identity? The *Merriam-Webster Dictionary* defines it like this:

I·den·ti·ty (n): Who someone is. . . .

Isn't that beautiful? I mean, think about it. Seriously give it some thought. I believe that most of us, me included, when asked what our identity is tend to throw out a list of accomplishments or hobbies, and label ourselves by those things.

"Yeah, well, I got like 237 likes on my selfie, so I guess that means I'm popular."

"I make good grades in school, so I guess you could say I'm smart."

"I'm the captain of the football team, so I would say that I'm an athlete."

These are all awesome things! I think likes on a selfie and having good grades are so cool. But are those answers good enough? Do they answer the question? The question wasn't "What do you do for fun?" or "What are you good at?" The question is so much more than that.

"What is your identity? Who are you?"

Now go back and read the definition of identity one more time.

Wow. That's heavy stuff. That question is floated around all the time. And if you're anything like me you answer it, or have answered it, by what you do, what you have done, or who you hang out with. Why?

Why do we find ourselves giving these superficial answers to such an awesomely huge question? If a person's identity is literally the fact of being who that person is, then a list of accomplishments or a friend group you're a part of isn't enough. Those answers are way too vague.

In order to find out the identity of something—who that something is—one must eventually look at how that something came about. The same is true with people. As a whole, our world is way too fixated on asking the finished product who or what they are. I want to argue that this is a hopelessly incomplete way to look at our identity. This way of trying to define ourselves is like looking at a painting and trying to figure out what the painter was trying to do while having absolutely zero knowledge about who the painter was.

Allow me to explain. If I look at the Mona Lisa and try my hardest to figure out what Leonardo da Vinci was trying to accomplish with this piece of art, I might start by staring at the canvas. I can

I·den·ti·ty (n):

Who someone is. . . .

notice the color palette, the composition, and the posing, and I can speculate on the subject's mysterious expression. But to fully understand who the woman was and why da Vinci painted her this way, I must step away from the painting and learn something about the artist.

In order to know the full meaning behind a painting we first must know the ways behind the painter. The painter knows the true meaning behind the painting because he is the one who created it. The same is true with people. We can learn a lot about someone by looking at their appearance, their habits, and their activities, but in order to know who or what we really are—our identity—we must learn about who created us: God.

The heartbeat behind this book is to help us fight the identity problem that is at the core of our self-image crisis by looking at who God tells us we are. Who God tells us we are has to be the center of our identity, because after all, He created us. Let's look at the very first description of man that God ever gave:

> *So God created man in his own image,*
> *in the image of God he created him;*
> *male and female he created them.*
> (Genesis 1:27, ESV)

In that one verse, in 22 short words, God gives us part of our core identity: images of Him.

For the rest of this book, we'll be exploring the ways that being made in God's image should change our lives. I am going to tell many different stories from my own life and try my best to be completely vulnerable with you. I pray that by the end of this book God does something incredible in your life, and you walk away from it knowing exactly who you are.

| | CH. 1 | |

CREATOR

When I was a little kid I loved watching my dad do things. It didn't matter what. I just liked watching him because he was my dad and I looked up to him. To give you a little insight on who my dad is, just picture Chuck Norris. Not quite that extreme, but pretty close. He grew a lot of our food in a massive garden that he made in the backyard. He taught my brother and me how to hunt for our own meat and then process it so we could eat it. We always had a freezer full of the meat that he would provide for our family through hunting and the crops that he would provide through gardening. Needless to say, I have always thought my dad was the coolest, toughest, and strongest guy I knew.

Watching him work in his garden was always so cool. He would walk down each row, starting with the tomatoes that were always on the left, and inspect them one by one. Then he would go to the collards, and the squash, and so on until he finished. Then he would wake up the next day and do it again. He knew his garden like the back of his hand. He created it and he then showed it love every single day. How could he not know it well?

My dad is also a phenomenal wood carver. He carves duck decoys by hand and then uses them to hunt. Carving them is clearly one of his favorite things to do. He would carve with insane concentration until he thought the decoy was good enough to display. Then he would get his paintbrushes and paint them in the most realistic way. He's an incredible artist and is so passionate about his work. I loved watching him get really excited about carving one and then hold it up periodically and ask me, "What do you think about that, boy?" I would always tell him I loved it.

I firmly believe that my dad can tell you every single detail about every decoy he has ever carved. He spends so much time working on them and he pours his heart into doing so. He still has several of them displayed around the house. He puts them up on the mantle or on the bookshelf as if to say, "I'm so proud of what I just created." After all, he did carve them by hand. How can he not be proud of that?

I believe that God does the same thing with us. He pours His heart into creating us and then He's proud of how we are made. He formed us each uniquely and purposefully, so just like my dad with his garden and his decoys, He knows every little detail about us. So let's pause to learn a little more about Him.

In Christianity, we believe that God is three distinct persons: the Father, the Son, and the Holy Spirit. This is called the Trinity. The thing that is so amazing about this is that the Father is not the Son, and the Son is not the Holy Spirit, and the Holy Spirit is not the Father, but they all make up one God. That's a huge concept to wrap your head around, I know. It's important, though, because it helps us understand exactly Who created us. Let's see what the gospel of John says about that:

> *In the beginning was the Word, and the Word was with God, and the Word was God. He was in the beginning with God. All things were made through him, and without him was not anything that was made.* (John 1:1–3, ESV)

I know what many of you may be thinking. "What is 'the Word,' and what does that have to do with creation?" It can be confusing, but let me explain.

How about instead of asking "what" the Word is, we ask "who" the Word is. Let's read on a bit further and we'll have our answer:

And the Word became flesh and dwelt among us, and we have seen his glory, glory as of the only Son from the Father, full of grace and truth. (John 1:14, ESV)

"The Word" in this passage is Jesus, the Son of God! He is the one who put on human flesh and came to live on Earth.

Now, look at verse 3 again:

All things were made through him, and without him was not anything that was made. (John 1:3, ESV)

This shows us that all things were made through Jesus. It says that without Jesus, nothing has ever been made. That means that not a single one of us was made without Jesus. So right there in five easy verses we see who our maker is—Jesus.

Hebrews 1:2 (ESV) shows us the same thing in a different way. It says,

But in these last days he [God the Father] has spoken to us by his Son [Jesus], whom he appointed the heir of all things, through whom also he created the world.

You know, in all the years I've been going to church, I have only heard two messages that talked about Jesus as our maker. Most messages only talk about how Jesus is our savior or how he's our friend. But when it comes to understanding our core identity, we first have to recognize who instilled that identity in each of us. This might seem elementary to some of you, but I have found it to be incredibly helpful to remember it in my own life. It has helped me realign my idea of who I am. I think about the decoys that my dad carves and how no two are the same. Each wooden replica of a duck lying around my parents' house is the way it is because of my dad—the one who made it. The same is true for us. We are all the way we are because of Jesus—the one who made us. When we recognize this daily and keep it at the forefront of our minds, we are able to walk into life's uncertainties with a certain clarity of who we are. That can make all the difference.

CREATION

Let's take a closer look at just how Jesus made us. On the first day of creation, God created the heavens and the earth; however, the earth was still without form and the Spirit of God hovered over the water. Then God said the famous line, "Let there be light," and light appeared into existence and He created night and day. Then the first day ended. On the second day, God called for an expanse in the waters to "separate the waters from the waters" (Genesis 1:6, ESV). And thus, the sky was created. Then it was the end of the second day.

On the third day God decided it was time to gather all of the water that He created into one place and for dry land to come up and separate some of these waters. He then called the land *Earth* and the water the *Seas*. He spoke trees and other vegetation into existence and gave them the ability to spread their seed. And as the third day was ending, God saw that what He created was *good*.

The fourth day comes and God creates the sun, the moon, and the stars. He saw that His work was *good*, and the fourth day came to a close.

On the fifth day, God decided it was time to put some life on Earth, outside of vegetation, so He created every living thing in the waters and every bird that flies in the air. He blessed them and told them to "be fruitful and multiply" (Genesis 1:22), or in other words, to reproduce. God enjoyed the work He did on the fifth day and He deemed it *good*.

On the sixth day of creation, God does something awesome. He decides to create all of the livestock and creatures on the Earth. He created every cow, dog, gorilla, anteater, and aardvark on this day. And then He said that the animals He had created were *good*.

Then God does something totally amazing. He creates mankind. And He deems His creation "very good" (Genesis 1:31).

Let's focus on this one amazing thing that Scripture tells us for a moment. After God created the plants and trees, the land and the fish, the birds and the livestock, even after He created the sun and the mountains, He said that what He had just made was *good.* But after he created man and woman, everything changed. Think about the mountains in Colorado for a second. Picture how they look when you drive by them, or fly over them, or snowboard down them. If you've never been, then think about the pictures of them that you've seen. Picture how beautiful they are in your mind. How they take your breath away and how you feel as if no picture from an iPhone X can even come close to capturing these mountains and all of their beauty.

Now picture the prettiest sunset you have ever seen. Maybe it was one when you were at the beach and the sun was setting over the calm, still, evening water. Or maybe it's one when you were on your family's farm and it goes down right over the open field that's behind the barn. Think about how it paints the sky. The different colors of red, yellow, and orange. Sometimes it even has some purple in it. It seems like it's straight out of a movie and that there is absolutely no way anything could ever be more spectacular than that sunset.

Now think about God on the day He created man. He had just seen the Earth take form a couple of days earlier. He witnessed the sun coming together and spoke light into it. He painted the mountains with His fingertips and was able to make them as beautiful as they are because He is the only one who can imagine something so spectacular and then actually create it. Think about God creating the heavens. He spoke the stars into existence and placed each one in a unique spot. He sees all of the beauty of the universe up close and personal because He created that beauty and it all flows from Him. But still, He thought that all of those things were simply "good."

Now think about this: when God created man and woman, everything was not "good" anymore. Instead, God now knew that everything was "very good."

I hope that you are letting that sink in right now. Because that was not just a one-time thing. God didn't only say that when he created Adam and Eve. When you were still in your mother's womb, all the way back to the time of conception, God was looking at you, molding you, creating you, and saying to Himself, "This is *very good*."

If we believe all that Scripture tells us about God then we believe He is perfect. That means that God doesn't make mistakes. God never messes up. Everything that God does, He does in the exact

When you were still

in your mother's womb,

all the way back

to the time of conception,

God was looking at you,

creating you,

and saying to Himself,

"This is *very good.*"

way He wants to. And that includes when He created you.

God looks at each of us and says, "You have been made so very good. Yes, the mountains are beautiful, and nobody could ever create a sunset like I do, but those things don't compare to you. You are so much more beautiful. You are my prize creation."

The fact that we are God's prize creation is something that is absolutely amazing to me. Every time I think about it I can't help but smile. It's something that I want to tell the whole world. Any time you begin to feel that you are anything less than God's prize creation, you should profess out loud the truth from God. Just say, "I have been made beautifully by my beautiful Maker, and I am a part of His prize creation."

The fact that Jesus looks at us and sees something beautiful is such an important truth that we need to grasp. Because the enemy loves to come into our lives and whisper in our ears that we aren't pretty enough. Or that we aren't tall enough. Or that our muscles are too small and that we have a little too much fat around our stomach. It's something that we all struggle with. It's a lie that Satan uses against all of us. He attempts to draw us away from the fact that our Creator sees us as beautiful.

PRAISE > PITY

The truth is that Jesus doesn't create faulty humans. He doesn't create anything less than beautiful. Yes, there are evil, evil people in this world. But they're not products of Jesus' lack of skill. They are products of Satan's lies. And although Jesus can't stand the sins that these evil people commit, He doesn't hate the people themselves.

Jesus loves everything and everyone He creates. Think about when you were a little kid and you were sitting in class and the teacher told you that it was time for arts and crafts. Remember how exciting that was? Remember how you couldn't wait to glue macaroni to a paper plate, or try your hardest to actually color in the lines? No matter what you made you always loved it. Why? Because you made it just how you wanted to.

When we were little kids we made our works of art in a way that we thought was beautiful. Sure, most of the time we strayed outside the lines or glued a little too much macaroni into one section of the paper. But you know what? We still loved what we had created. We still brought it home, showed our families, and hoped that it got put up on the refrigerator for everyone to see. We didn't care how the world viewed our creation, because to us, all that mattered was how we viewed it. Don't you think Jesus does the same thing with us?

So think about how you treasured all of the things you created as a child. It didn't matter if they weren't the perfect shape or if they were a little bit lop-sided. You loved them anyway because they looked exactly how you wanted them to look. Now imagine how much greater that feeling is for Jesus, because He didn't just glue macaroni on a paper plate. He created life. He formed you inside of your mother exactly how He wanted to and He calls you beautiful and loved. David paints a beautiful picture of this in Psalm 139:13–15 (ESV):

For you formed my inward parts;
you knitted me together in my mother's womb.
I praise you, for I am fearfully and wonderfully
*   made.*
Wonderful are your works;
my soul knows it very well.
My frame was not hidden from you,
when I was being made in secret,
intricately woven in the depths of the earth.

Those words are words of a man who knows how incredible his Maker is. David couldn't help but write praise about Him! He knew who created him, and because of that he knew who he was. He knew that he was fearfully and wonderfully made. He walked in confidence knowing that God's works were wonderful. Not just some of them, but all of them. Setting our eyes on our Maker instead of ourselves allows us to praise Him for all that He is instead of pity ourselves for all that we aren't.

I all too often see people bash themselves so hard for their flaws that they completely discount the power of God. It's as if they have blinders on, and the only thing they allow themselves to focus on are the parts of themselves that they don't like. Things like their personality, their weight, their failures. . . . I have noticed that when our perception turns from focusing inwardly on our flaws to outwardly on God's perfection and power, it will radically change our lives. Where does your perception focus?

Recognizing who my Maker was changed my life. It has changed me from a hollow shell of a boy who wallowed in self-pity to a deeply rich man who praises the One who made him. And I promise, praise is so much greater than pity.

MANKIND

I love that humans were made specially by God, not accidently evolved from other mammals. The greatest thing about this is that our beauty doesn't come from the world, but from God. We see this in Genesis 2 during the creation of mankind:

When no bush of the field was yet in the land and no small plant of the field had yet sprung up—for the LORD God had not caused it to rain

*on the land, and there was no man to work the
ground, and a mist was going up from the land
and was watering the whole face of the
ground—then the LORD God formed the man of
dust from the ground and breathed into his
nostrils the breath of life, and the man became a
living creature. And the LORD God planted a
garden in Eden in the east, and there he put the
man who he had formed.* (Genesis 2:5–8, ESV)

I don't know how you feel about that, but it
seems a little more intense than staying in the lines
of a coloring book to me. I mean, God literally created man from dust. And He created man exactly
how He wanted to. In every way He thought that
His creation of man was "very good." And you
know what the best part is? Nowhere in Scripture
does it ever say,

And God looked at the man he just created
and saw that he had a six-pack and was 6
feet, 2 inches tall with an amazing jaw line
and clear skin, and declared that his creation was very good.

No, it doesn't say that anywhere. Instead it just
simply says,

*The LORD God formed the man of dust from the
ground and breathed into his nostrils the breath
of life, and the man became a living creature.*
(Genesis 2:7, ESV)

There was no need for God to talk about the physical characteristics of Adam. Why? Because they didn't matter to God. God was more focused on who Adam was at his core than how Adam looked on the outside. God created Adam for a purpose, and I can promise you that it wasn't to be "hot."

God made Adam to work the Earth He had just created. He wanted him to steward the animals of the land and the birds of the air. He also wanted him to work in the fields and take care of His garden. God created Adam to live for Him, his Creator, not to live for the world and its standards. I think it is safe to say that we have lost sight of this.

Let's look at what happens a few verses later in Genesis 2 and see if we can find something different when God created woman:

> *The man gave names to all livestock and to the birds of the heavens and to every beast of the field. But for Adam there was not a helper fit for him. So the LORD God caused a deep sleep to fall upon the man, and while he slept took one of his ribs and closed up its place with flesh. And the rib that the LORD God had taken from the man he made into a woman and brought her to the man.* (Genesis 2:20–22, ESV)

I studied this scripture for a while during the writing of this chapter. I looked over it time and time again and tried to find something that said the woman was beautiful because "She was skinny." I even looked for it to mention the woman being beautiful because she was "curvy." But guess what . . . I couldn't find anything.

Nowhere in the passages about God creating humans does it say anything about their beauty from a worldly viewpoint. Why would it? If God thought that being beautiful meant you were skinny, tall, had clear skin, or a nice body, then He would have said that. He sees us as what we are— His creations that He knows are incredibly beautiful just because they are His.

THE PRAYER

My prayer is that this realization changes someone's viewpoint of their self like it has mine. I pray that it transforms someone's life from a struggle of self-pity to a journey of praise. I encourage you to look at your Maker instead of yourself, because only then can you see your true beauty.

I pray that you use this knowledge to fight off lies from the enemy. Next time Satan is trying to get inside your head and tell you that you aren't good enough because of the way you look, try reading Psalm 139 or Genesis 1–2. Let the absolute truth from God kill all of the lies that Satan will try to feed you. At the end of the day Satan can't change who we are, but only who we think we are.

I pray that you set your gaze on Jesus. If we keep a constant reminder within ourselves that God has made us wonderfully and beautifully, then we will begin to live in a new light that is brighter and more fulfilling than any other light we could ever imagine.

| | CH. 2 | |

JESUS: GOD

It is so easy for us to allow things of this world to define us. They are so tangible. We see them and know a lot about them, and because of this we tend to let them take up a bigger portion of our life than we should. One of the ways I see this most often is when people define themselves by the friends that they have. They might be in with the popular crowd and base their entire life around the fact that they have the right friends. Or they might be in the outcast group, and think of themselves as a loser because they don't have that many friends. It's so easy to fall into those traps because of how well we can see them. It's obvious to see that we either have friends or we don't. It's easy to see that our grades are either really good, or not the best. It's clear that we are either athletic, or not at all. It's so easy to let those things define us because of how much we know about them. For me, I fell into a trap of defining myself strictly based on how I performed in sports. It took up literally every thought in my mind. I was consumed by being the best, lifting the most, and living up to everyone's expectations for me. We'll talk more about this later on.

Generally speaking, the things that define us are, more often than not, the things that we are the most familiar with. Many people who define themselves by their past mistakes spend a huge chunk of their day thinking about them (also me). Or people who define themselves by their work usually spend the majority of their time working (I've been here before, too). It's so easy for people to fall into these traps, and I have been the poster child for this. Familiarity breeds the opportunity for us to get stuck in what we know.

I believe that our identity doesn't come from what we do. It can't come from our work or our friend group, because those things are shallow and will eventually fade away. Our identity has to come from a constant—which is God. As we saw in the last chapter, He made us through His Son Jesus, so our true identity is found in the person of Jesus. So if it is true that the things that define us are usually the things that we are the most familiar with, then it is imperative for us to become more familiar with Jesus.

Before we look at some practical aspects of our identity in later chapters, we must first look at Jesus. We need to explore who He is and what His life on Earth was all about. In doing this, hopefully you will see how He has the ability to define who you are.

GOD

We looked at John 1 in the last chapter to see that Jesus is God, but let's take another look:

In the beginning was the Word, and the Word was with God, and the Word was God. He was in the beginning with God. (John 1:1–2, ESV)

We learned that the Word is Jesus, the second Person of the Trinity, the Son of God. So if you read John 1:1–2 again, you can substitute "the Word" with "Jesus," and it reads like this:

In the beginning was Jesus, and Jesus was with God, and Jesus was God. He was in the beginning with God.

Isn't that amazing? Jesus is 100 percent God. The pure divinity of Jesus is something that has made me cry multiple times throughout any given week. It's one of a kind. It's perfect. It's what makes Jesus the most extraordinary and extravagant Being in existence. Let's take a look at some of the miracles Jesus performed to see just how truly divine He really is.

LIGHT ALWAYS WINS

One remarkable miracle is described in the book of Mark. Mark is an awesome book in the Bible and I believe that chapter five is one of the greatest chapters in the entire book. I heard one of my favorite communicators, a man named Ben Stuart, give a talk on this chapter while I was at a retreat for high school students. I believe that Ben explained the events I want to write about in such a strong and powerful way. In fact, I'm not sure I have ever heard them taught better. Because of this, I'm going to write about Mark 5 in a similar way to how Ben taught it on it that day.

To give you a little bit of context to this passage of Scripture, Jesus had just finished calming a storm that was about to kill all of His disciples while they were sailing across a large body of water. As you can imagine, the disciples were blown away, and probably very scared, because of Jesus.

So chapter five starts when they finally land the boat on the other side of the sea in the country of the Gerasenes. Scripture tells us that immediately as Jesus stepped out of the boat, a man with an unclean spirit started running at Him from out of the tombs. This wasn't just some regular guy with an unclean spirit. Scripture tells us that this joker was mean. It tells us that he was strong. It even tells us that he lived among the tombs, or in other words, he lived with dead people. This guy was no joke.

The man with the unclean spirit had lived among the dead for years. Scripture tells us that people used to bind him up and tie him down with shackles and chains, but that the man became too strong and he "wrenched the chains apart, and he broke the shackles into pieces." (Mark 5:4b, ESV) It says that nobody had the strength to subdue him. This guy would stay up at night in the tombs and scream while he cut himself with stones.

Let's just imagine how the disciples were feeling at this point. They were coming off the boat scared out of their minds because they were almost killed by a deadly storm, but then Jesus had told the storm to stop, and it listened. Then as soon as they start walking on dry land again, this man with an unclean spirit who wrenched chains and broke shackles starts running toward them. I can imagine that they were probably thinking, "It is about to go down." I mean, come on. I'm sure we would all be thinking the same thing. Jesus just quieted a storm and this man with an unclean spirit broke iron and lived with dead people. Everybody there was ready to see the throwdown of the century.

But that's not at all what happened. Mark 5:6–8 (ESV) says:

And when he [the man] saw Jesus from afar, he ran and fell down before him. And crying out with a loud voice, he said, "What have you to do with me, Jesus, Son of the Most High God? I

> *adjure you by God, do not torment me." For he [Jesus] was saying to him, "Come out of the man, you unclean spirit!"*

This "throwdown of the century" that I'm sure people were expecting to see turned out completely different. This man, the same one who broke shackles to pieces and whom nobody had the strength to subdue, charged toward Jesus just so he could wallow at his feet and beg him not to torment him.

My favorite thing that Ben Stuart said came after he talked about how the unclean spirit fell at Jesus' feet. He said, "You see, there is no fight here. Light always wins."

This is so incredible because it shows us the true Godliness of Jesus. The man with an unclean spirit wasn't fully human; he was possessed by a demon that was for the darkness and against the light. He was aided by a supernatural being who only had the intentions of destroying him. So this man, who had a strong supernatural being inside of him, begged at Jesus' feet for mercy. He didn't even try to put up a fight. Why? Because he knew who Jesus was. He knew He was the Son of the Most High God. He knew that Jesus was God in the flesh.

The story later plays out with Jesus casting the demon that was inside the man into a herd of pigs. But the true nature of who Jesus was shined in that moment. In that one day, Jesus calmed a storm that

"You see,

there is no fight here.

Light always wins."

—Ben Stuart

was about to kill all of His friends, and a demon-possessed man who surpassed all others in strength wallowed at His feet. In that one day, people witnessed how Jesus was 100 percent God.

PERFECTLY PERFECT

Many more passages in Scripture show us the divinity of Jesus. Scripture tells us He walked on water, that He walked through walls, and that the heavens opened up after He was baptized and the Holy Spirit came upon Him in the shape of a dove. It tells us that He was perfect. It tells us that He can make all things new. Nothing can stain who Jesus is. He ate with sinners yet never sinned. He was beaten and hung on a cross, but not one of His bones was broken. He even walked with lepers and didn't get sick.

I mean, come on. Leprosy? That's an ugly, ugly disease. Those who had leprosy in Jesus' time were ordered into exile and forced to leave the city. They weren't allowed to get close to anyone, and everywhere they went they had to shout "unclean" so that people knew not to go near them. They would quickly become second-class citizens.

Leprosy often caused people to lose their fingers. Chunks of their skin would rot and fall off. They looked like actual zombies. And as we all can imagine, the disease was painful. It was excruciating. It was one of the worst things that could happen to you if you lived during that time. There was no cure for it. If you contracted leprosy, then you were almost certainly going to die.

One of the many different things that made leprosy so dangerous was how contagious it was. If you even brushed up against someone who had it, then chances were you were going to get it too. That is why the people who had leprosy had to leave the city and shout that they were sick to everyone. Everything they touched became unclean. Nobody wanted to come close to them. Nobody but Jesus.

In Luke 5 we see an incredible display of Jesus' love, compassion, and divinity.

> *While he [Jesus] was in one of the cities, there came a man full of leprosy. And when he saw Jesus, he fell on his face and begged him, "Lord, if you will, you can make me clean." And Jesus stretched out his hand and touched him, saying, "I will; be clean." And immediately the leprosy left him.* (Luke 5:12–13, ESV)

Isn't it incredible that the touch from the leper didn't make Jesus unclean—but instead the touch from Jesus made the leper completely healed? If it were any other person who touched that man, they probably would have feared for their life. But Jesus wasn't just some man. He was God.

God is so perfect that not a single thing can make him unclean. Not even a touch from a man with leprosy. But instead, God's touch can make all things new. Just like what happened to the leper and just like what has happened to many of us.

THE PRAYER

In recognizing the fact that Jesus our Creator was 100 percent God, we can see how He has the ability—even the right—to define us. Who else could really define us other than the One who created us?

I pray that as we walk through the pages of this book together, Jesus opens your eyes to see who you really are. I pray that we all come to realize that He is the only one who can give us our core identity. I pray that all of our perceptions become outwardly focused on a perfect God who has the power to speak life into existence and has never made a mistake.

| | CH. 3 | |

JESUS: HUMAN

It started with one drink at a party in high school. I thought about it for a second, and then decided that one drink wouldn't hurt. Three hours later, and after about six drinks, I could hardly stand up. That night started something that led me down a path to the darkest time in my life.

After that first night of drinking, I started doing it a little more regularly with some friends. I thought to myself that if I drank every once in a while, and in moderation, it couldn't cause that much harm. Well, at 16 years old, I never could've imagined the road it would lead me on. After a couple of months of drinking casually with some friends, I started doing it a little more. I would drink on Friday nights after football games, and then again on Saturday nights when I would go to my friend's house. My casual drinking turned into binge drinking seemingly overnight. Eventually I wasn't willing or able to have fun unless alcohol was involved.

When I was drinking heavily in high school, it changed who I was. I was angrier at people. I didn't care about others' feelings. I just wanted to have fun and drink. It caused me to be lazy in school, and I couldn't perform in athletics the way I wanted to. My drinking started as something that I saw as harmless—just one or two drinks casually with some friends. Then it grew into a darkness that surrounded my entire life without me even knowing it.

Temptation is dangerous. It softens us up with the idea that it's not that bad, then it wraps its arms around our throat and chokes the life right out of us. But the good news is that we have a defense against temptation and a God who understands it.

BEATING TEMPTATION

One of the biggest misconceptions about Jesus is that He doesn't understand us. We believe that He just looks down from heaven and shakes His head and says, "Guys . . . it's not that hard." We see Him as just some watchman who doesn't know what it's like to be a teenager going through puberty. We don't appreciate that He was ever tired, hungry, thirsty, frustrated, angry, sad, or any other

Jesus' life on Earth

didn't separate us

from Him at all;

it's what brought us closer.

emotion or feeling that has a negative connotation. We see Jesus' life on Earth as something that separates us from Him because of the impossibility that we could ever live our lives the same way. We couldn't be more wrong. Jesus' life on Earth didn't separate us from Him at all; it's what brought us closer.

The reason we don't believe Jesus understands us is because we don't understand how much we have in common with Him. We don't understand that not only was He fully God, but He was also fully man. That is so overlooked by people, but it's one of the unique components of Jesus' life that makes it so beautiful.

The only thing I can compare this to is the countless number of fights that teenagers get in with their parents because they "don't understand them." I mean, how many times have we all experienced that? We wanted to do something, our parents said no, and we got mad at them and proceeded to inform them that they don't know what it's like to be "young and in love." Or that they don't realize the pressure that is on teenagers to perform well in school. Or that they've had the same careers forever, so they could never understand how hard it is to find a job after college.

The problem with this argument is that our parents haven't always been old people who have their lives all together. There was a time when our parents were "young and in love." They've struggled in school. They've wanted to go hang out with friends, but their parents didn't let them. And believe it or not, they haven't always known what they wanted to do with their lives.

The truth for a lot of us is that nobody on Earth understands what you're going through better than your parents. They've lived through all of the things that you are going through now, or that you went through when you were a kid. And the same is true with Jesus. He isn't tucked away in heaven confused about what you're struggling with. Jesus has been on the front lines of life and has experienced so much of what we experience. He was made fun of, hated on, beat up, cast out, and even tempted. He understands what it's like to have the devil whisper in His ear and tempt Him. He knows what it feels like to be upset with His friends. He's been frustrated and angry, and at one time He even flipped over a bunch of tables (in the most righteous way possible). However, one of the major things that separates us from Jesus is how He responded to all of it.

Matthew 4 gives an incredible account of Jesus' face-to-face encounter with the devil:

Then Jesus was led up by the Spirit into the wilderness to be tempted by the devil. And after fasting forty days and forty nights, he was hungry. And the tempter came and said to him,

"If you are the son of God, command these stones to become loaves of bread." But he answered, "It is written, 'Man shall not live by bread alone, but by every word that comes from the mouth of God.'"

Then the devil took him to the holy city and set him on the pinnacle of the temple and said to him, "If you are the Son of God, throw yourself down, for it is written, 'He will command his angels concerning you,' and 'On their hands they will bear you up, lest you strike your foot against a stone.'"

Jesus said to him, "Again it is written, 'You shall not put the Lord your God to the test.'" Again the devil took him to a very high mountain and showed him all the kingdoms of the world and their glory. And he said to him, "All these I will give you, if you will fall down and worship me." Then Jesus said to him, "Be gone, Satan! For it is written, 'You shall only worship the Lord your God and him only shall you serve.'"

Then the devil left him, and behold, angels came and were ministering to him.
(Matthew 4:1–11, ESV)

This passage of Scripture tells us a lot of different things. However, I think that one of the most comforting things it tells us is that Jesus was tempted, just like us. It tells us that He got hungry, just like us. And it tells us that He got angry, just like us.

We can clearly see that Jesus was tempted by the devil in this passage. In fact, the devil audibly spoke to Jesus face-to-face in this time of temptation. I think most of us can say that we have never been tempted that intensely. The most beautiful part of this passage is that not only does it show us that Jesus was tempted and that He knows what we're going through when we face the same thing, but it also shows us how we should handle that temptation. When the devil spoke to Jesus and told him that He could have the entire world as His kingdom if He just worshiped him, Jesus didn't sit there and say, "no thanks." He didn't passively run away and hope the devil didn't follow him. When the devil spoke to Jesus and told Him the lie that it's better to have all of the kingdoms on Earth than to worship God, Jesus responded with truth.

Scripture calls the devil the king of lies, which means that he will always tell us lies when tempting us, just like he did with Jesus. And Jesus showed us that the best way to fight the king of lies is with absolute truth from God. The truth Jesus responded with was Scripture that He knew countered what the devil was saying. Jesus shows us right then and there that one of the best ways to fight temptation is by quoting Scripture, which is the truth from God Himself. It makes sense, right?

So not only does Jesus understand what it's like to be a human who gets tempted, but He also knows what it takes to be a human who beats temptation. I don't know about you, but I think it's so comforting to have a savior who has put on human flesh and has defeated the very things I face every single day. This allows us to be courageous in how we fight temptation. It allows us to be bold in how we speak about Jesus. It allows us to be victorious over the struggles in our lives. Why? Because Jesus was victorious first.

VALIDATION

So yes, Jesus was tempted. He became angry. He got hungry, tired, and annoyed. But He also was friendly. He was nice. He had relationships and loved people better than anyone who has ever lived. Jesus laughed. He experienced immense joy. Jesus even rejoiced because of how happy he was about others' salvation. Jesus' emotional highs and lows are all throughout the Gospels.

For all you article readers out there, I recommend looking up the article "Jesus Is Fully Human" by David Mathis, who is the executive editor for DesiringGod.org and a pastor at Cities Church in Minneapolis. Mathis writes a couple of paragraphs in this article that I believe beautifully illustrate how Jesus was fully man:

It is clear enough from the New Testament that Jesus has a human body. John 1:14 means at least this, and more: "The Word became flesh." Jesus' humanity is one of the first tests of orthodoxy (1 John 4:2; 2 John 7). Jesus was born (Luke 2:7). He grew (Luke 2:40, 52). He grew tired (John 4:6) and got thirsty (John 19:28) and hungry (Matthew 4:2). He became physically weak (Matthew 4:11; Luke 23:26). He died (Luke 23:46). And he had a real human body after his resurrection (Luke 24:39; John 20:20, 27).

Throughout the Gospels, Jesus clearly displays human emotions. When Jesus heard the centurion's words of faith, "he marveled" (Matthew 8:10). He says in Matthew 26:38 that his "soul is very sorrowful, even to death." In John 11:33–35, Jesus is "deeply moved in his spirit and greatly troubled" and even weeps. In John 12:27 He says, "Now is my soul troubled," and in John 13:21, He is "troubled in his spirit." The author to the Hebrews writes that "Jesus offered up prayers and supplications, with loud cries and tears." (Hebrews 5:7) John Calvin memorably summed it up: "Christ has put on our feelings along with our flesh."

If you still don't believe me, or Mr. Mathis, that Jesus experienced some of these distinctly human emotions and problems, then feel free to study the Scriptures for yourself. Matthew, Mark, Luke, and

John are the four Gospel accounts of Jesus' life that are in the Bible, and they offer some awesome insight as to how Jesus was 100 percent man. Some passages that you might want to start off studying are Matthew 21:12–16, John 11:1–44, and Mark 3:1–6.

PRAY

One thing that we can learn about Jesus was how He spent his time on Earth. The vast majority of records we have on Jesus are about the last three years of His life. During this time, He treated people with radical and passionate love. He spoke to massive crowds and healed and fed thousands. He mentored a select few and walked through life with them. But perhaps one of the most incredible aspects of Jesus' life is that He still needed time alone with God.

In the last chapter, we read a story from Luke 5 about how Jesus healed a man with leprosy. After Jesus did this, His fame grew exponentially, and Scripture tells us that great crowds gathered to hear Him and be healed of their illnesses. As you can imagine, this was exhausting. So Luke 5:16 (ESV) tells us this:

> But he [Jesus] would withdraw into desolate places and pray.

Jesus, being completely human, needed to spend alone time to pray to His Father. He needed to rest and be rejuvenated. He longed to praise His Father. Jesus was no longer in heaven sitting on the right-hand side of the Father, so He longed for that alone time with Him. If Jesus, who is God in human flesh, needed time to retreat and pray to God the Father, then so do we.

THE PRAYER

Since Jesus was 100 percent human, he knows what it takes to be a perfect human. Nobody has ever been more qualified to tell us who we are than the only perfect person ever to live. Jesus under-stands us. He's been in our shoes. He knows what it's like to fight temptation and to be tired. He knows what it's like to be hated and beaten. He lived on Earth as a human, but even then he was still God. Completely, fully, and wonderfully God.

I pray that we let the weight of this truth sink into our everyday lives. It has the power to encour-age you and propel you forward into life's uncertainties because you know you won't be tak-ing them on alone. You have a God on your side who knows what the situation feels like. Who has been there before, and who conquered it long ago.

| | CH. 4 | |

CONSTANT

When I was in kindergarten I had my first encounter with a bully. His name was William and he was a monstrous five-year-old. I still vividly remember the day I met him for the very first time.

It was time for recess and I was playing outside on the jungle gym with a few of my friends when this kid that I didn't recognize walked by. All I was thinking about was how was he so much bigger than everyone else. I kind of stared at him for a few seconds then went back to playing. Later, a few of us decided it was time to see how fast we could run up the slide, so we headed off for the main playground set. We were having a good ol' time, just minding our own business and falling off the slide every once in a while, when I felt this gut-wrenching feeling in the pit of my stomach. I caught something massive charging at me out of the corner of my eye. It was William sprinting towards me with a facial expression that clearly said, "I'm going to kill you." I didn't know what to do so I just took off running. Luckily, I was the fastest kid in my grade and he never caught me, but at that point it became clear that any hopes I had of adding William to my list of friends were out of the picture.

This went on every day at recess for several months. It was like a never-ending chase that happened at 1:15 every afternoon, Monday through Friday. I would be minding my own business and then here comes William. It almost became game-like. You know, if there was a game called try not to get beat up. I never found out why William wanted to hurt me so bad, but I think it had something to with a girl. Who knows? But whatever the reason was, he sure did hate me.

You know how when you look back at your childhood and you try to remember certain events but you simply can't? You try to remember when you learned to tie your shoes, but for whatever reason, the memory just doesn't seem to be there? That's how it is for the day William and I became friends. I have distinct memories of how he used to chase me around the playground, and then my memory fast-forwards to walking to his house after school to spend the night as good friends.

Somehow along the way, William's perception of me changed drastically. He went from wanting to give me wedgies at recess to being my absolute best friend for nearly 20 years. One thing that I have learned from how William and I became friends is that it is human nature to be inconsistent. Humans change. We are constantly changing our minds about most things in our lives. It's like our perception of certain things has a running clock, and when that clock hits zero it's time for our perception to change. As I know to be true from my friendship with William, our perception of people changes. Our taste in music changes. Our favorite food changes. What we believe to be beautiful changes.

YOUNG LOVE

The first time I ever realized that someone's personal perception of beauty could change was the summer going into my junior year of high school. There was this girl that was a year ahead of me in school, and I had grown up knowing of her my entire life. Her name was Amber. She was pretty much the girl in school that all of the guys wanted to date. Except for me; I'm not sure why not.

My sister was best friends with her sister, so we would run into each other every now and then growing up, but we were never really friends. William used to have a huge crush on her, as did everyone else in my school, but for some reason I never liked her. I would always say, "She's just not really my type." Then summer going into junior year happened, and man . . . did I eat my words then. Amber and I hung out in a group setting a couple of times, and I realized that she was actually extremely cool. So I did what every small-town 16-year-old boy would do; I invited her over to my house and we ate fried chicken sandwiches while watching a movie. Suddenly I was hooked on this girl. I didn't see her as just one of my sister's friend's sisters anymore. In my eyes, she had suddenly become the most beautiful girl in Griffin, Georgia.

Amber and I kind of had a "thing" off and on for a good while her senior year and the summer going into her freshman year of college. We were never boyfriend and girlfriend, but people knew that we were into each other. But as I mentioned earlier, perceptions of people change. She went off to the University of Georgia and we tried to stay in touch the best we could, but it had become clear to me that the way she viewed me had changed. She stopped seeing me as a potential boyfriend and started viewing me as just a buddy. And just like that, her perception of me had changed.

For whatever reason, my perception of this girl that grew up less than a mile from me and whom I had seen all my life changed too. I went from thinking that she wasn't my type to being head over heels for her for the next two years. But as they do, my fickle human emotions and perceptions changed again, and I got over Amber. What at the time seemed like a world-ending event ended up being a simple life lesson and an opportunity to grow. I went off to college, and after a year of being completely single I met the most amazing girl. Her name is Madeline and she has challenged me, loved me, and encouraged me for the last few years. We are now married and I couldn't be happier.

We see this happen all the time in high school relationships. People meet someone and fall "madly in love" and swear that they are getting married. However, as soon as the quarterback gets injured, his best friend the fullback starts looking better and better (*Friday Night Lights* reference). High school relationships prove that humans are consistently inconsistent. When people grow up and get married, they begin to be inconsistent in other ways. Some of us can speak to that better than others.

VARIABLES

Perhaps one of the best examples of human inconsistency is found in the world of sports. There is this incredible disease that happens to so many sports fans every single year. It's called the bandwagon effect: when a sports fan decides to stop rooting for one team in order to root for another because the other team is doing so well. It's actually quite disturbing. Many of these fans have been loyal to one team throughout their entire life, but the moment they saw Steph Curry's 2015–2016 season they quickly dropped the Hawks. That last sentence might have had some bitterness in it, but I'm just trying to prove my point.

I say all of that to point out that there are very few things in this world that humans remain constant with. It seems like people now have a new boyfriend or girlfriend every time you see them, and your buddy down the road wasn't a Panthers fan until last week. But this is not a new phenomenon. Throughout history humans have changed their minds and have been consistently inconsistent. We can see this in wars where one nation decides to start fighting against an ally nation. It's present in government, from people believing that a monarchy is ideal and then overthrowing their king and adopting a democracy. And it's especially true regarding the changing perception of beauty.

If you don't believe that the perception of what is beautiful has changed over time, then chances are you don't remember early middle school. But that's just one example. In the 1600s, the most "beautiful" females were what modern America calls overweight. It was also all the rage for the men to wear makeup and put on big, over-the-top wigs. Dressing like this as a man, or being bigger as a woman, was a sign that you were in good health and well-off financially—which was an attractive thing to be. More recently than the 1600s, things have changed a lot during just the last 70 years in America.

In the 1950s, the ideal woman was curvy. This was when Marilyn Monroe was the most famous woman in America, and she epitomized what was thought of as perfect beauty in this time. People also believed curly hair and peachy cheeks to be beautiful. However, if you fast-forward just ten years to the 1960s, the perception of a perfect body image had changed drastically. Being curvy was no longer in, but instead the most beautiful women were rail thin and had big eyelashes. The perception of beauty shifted from having curves and peachy cheeks, to being extremely slim and having strong facial expressions. Those are extremely different body types, and that perception shifted in a span of just ten years. The trend of changing perception of beauty moved into the 1970s, 80s, and 90s. Each had their own variation of what was believed to be beautiful at the time, from platform shoes and polyester, to shoulder pads and perms, to shredded jeans and plaid.

The earthly perception of what is beautiful doesn't just change over time, but it's also different in just about every culture across the globe. What is considered to be beautiful in Mexico is most likely not going to be considered to be beautiful in China. For example, young white women in the United States now generally believe that the ideal body image is thin and tanned. By contrast, a 2015 study from Sudan showed that more than two-thirds of young women bleach their skin to make it lighter. The harmful effects of skin bleaching are pretty intense, but they don't seem to care. Meanwhile, in the United States, many young women go to tanning salons to make their skin darker. The harmful effects of tanning are pretty intense, but they don't seem to care. Why? In both cases, it's because they are trapped in a false reality in which they believe that their body is supposed to correlate with their culture's perspective of beauty.

Back in Sudan, researchers also found that the majority of young women will force-feed themselves, even when they're not hungry, in order to gain weight. In their culture, the perfect body shape is one with a heavier build. So the young women of Sudan will eat until they physically can't any longer in order to meet that expectation of having a "perfect body." In the United States, it is the complete opposite. The American cultural perception of the perfect body image is one that is thin and "in shape." So many young women (and men) will keep themselves from eating. They will starve themselves in order to live up to the expectation that they have to look a certain way. I have had countless people in my life suffer from eating disorders because of what society and culture told them was "beautiful." But I don't think any of them realized just how different each culture's perception of beauty is.

I'm ready for the day when people don't go to tanning beds, or starve themselves, or bleach their skin, because they feel like they have to meet certain criteria in how they look. Because chances are, in 30 years, being tan, thin, and in shape won't be the "best" way to look. Why? Because worldly perception of what is beautiful is always changing. We should never rely on something that is variable to make us happy. We should never rely on something that is variable to bring us self-worth. Because at some point or another, that variable will vary. And when it does you will be left broken, disappointed, and with a feeling of no self-worth. And because the world's perspective on what is beautiful is always changing, we will never be able to keep living up to those expectations. As soon as we think we fit the mold of what society calls beautiful, then it will be time for that mold to change again. We will be trapped in a never-ending chase after something that we will never be able to obtain.

STRENGTH FROM GRACE

The opposite of something that is always changing is something that never changes. Or in more mathematical terms, the opposite of a variable is a constant. It is clear that worldly perception of beauty is a variable. By contrast, we find in Scripture that our God is a God who never changes. He is the same now as he was 10,000 years ago and he will stay that way forever. I believe that two of the most comforting verses in Scripture are Hebrews 13:8–9. It's a popular couple of verses, and for good reason. They read:

> *Jesus Christ is the same yesterday and today and forever. Do not be led away by diverse and strange teachings, for it is good for the heart to be strengthened by grace, not by foods, which have not benefited those devoted to them.* (ESV)

Wow. What a powerful two verses. The fact that Jesus, who is our Savior, our Lord, and our Creator, is the same today as He was yesterday and as He will be forever is the most amazing thing. I also believe that verse 9 is completely appropriate for what we are talking about. I love how it says:

> *For it is good for the heart to be strengthened by grace, not by foods, which have not benefited those devoted to them.*

The writer is talking about how we should not listen to false teachings, specifically, doctrines about certain foods to eat. The fact is that these doctrines are manmade. They are an old system based on people being "good enough" by following rules instead of on people living freely in grace. I think that today's society mirrors these doctrines with different things. Instead of certain foods, people are only "good enough" if they have a certain body shape. Or if they have a certain friend group. Or if they have certain grades. But just like the foods in Hebrews 13:9, people have not benefited in the long run when they are devoted to living up to the world's standards.

Hebrews 13:8 means that we will always have a steady foundation to stand on. It means that we will always have something constant to believe in. We will have something constant to find our self-worth and identity in. That means we can stop running in this never-ending chase to live up to earthly expectations and perceptions that are always changing. Instead we can look at our Creator, see who He is and who He tells us we are, and then live freely in that never-changing truth forever.

COUNTER-CULTURE

The fact that God is constant is one of my favorite things. There are times where I am reading Scripture during a quiet time and I forget that the

God I serve is the same God whose story I'm reading. I think it is so easy for us to look at the stories in the Old Testament and tell ourselves that since all of that happened thousands of years ago, it couldn't possibly be relevant to our lives today. Or we can read the New Testament and tell ourselves that since the world has changed so much in the last 2,000 years, it's acceptable for us to live differently than how the Bible says to. Or we look at everyone else in our culture, or country, or school, or sports team and see how they are living their lives, and we fall into this trap of thinking that the Bible just hasn't caught up with our culture yet. This way of thinking is one of the easiest traps to fall into in modern-day Christianity. But at the same time it's also one of the most inaccurate and insulting. Not insulting to Christians, but to God. Now I'm not sure about you, but thinking that I might insult God scares the crap out of me.

Many of us have formed this belief that since the world has changed, the Bible should change too. We think that since culture says something is okay, the Bible must not be right anymore. We treat Scripture like we can amend certain things that we don't agree with or things that modern society opposes. The most common example of this that I have seen in the last several years is Christians who think it is okay to live with their boyfriend or girlfriend before they're married. I hear them justify it

We can look at our Creator,

see who He is

and who He tells us we are,

and then live freely

in that never-changing truth

forever.

with, "Well, the rest of the world does it, and they're all really good people." Or they say the classic excuse, "The Bible was written for the specific time frame and culture of thousands of years ago. Some of that stuff just doesn't have a place in our world."

I believe that one of the most arrogant things someone who claims to love God can believe is that God's Word needs to "catch up" with culture. I understand non-Christians who think this way, but not people who consider themselves Jesus-followers. Now please, don't get me wrong. I'm not condemning everyone who has a live-in boyfriend or girlfriend; I'm just proclaiming the truth. I'm not here to discredit anyone's faith or anything like that. God gives grace freely, but we can't take advantage of that grace by continuing to live in sin. The main thing I am trying to say here is that God's word is constant. His love is never-changing and He Himself is the same way. As Jesus-followers, we should all believe this. That means that the argument that says certain things in the Bible do not apply to our culture is completely wrong.

COMFORT IN THE CONSISTENCY

The fact that the God we serve is a constant God is something we should all hold on to. If we look at how modern America operates, then we can see that almost all of the foundations that people build their self-worth and identity on are unstable. For example, the stock market: Men who are very successful stockbrokers and who make a lot of money for years can lose it all in one day. That turns the very successful stockbroker, who has only identified himself as successful and rich, into not so successful and definitely not rich. Then, more times than not, he will question everything he's done in his life that brought him up to that point, and he will feel like a failure to his family, friends, and co-workers. Or take another example, outward appearance: Girls who define themselves as the pretty and popular girls for years will one day find themselves old and wrinkly. If they have only identified themselves in terms of, and only been celebrated for, their superficial beauty, they will start to feel lost, empty, and alone because they found their self-worth in a variable.

Living a life defined by variables is a problem we all have. It's easy to fall into. However, it causes a feeling of uneasiness because deep inside each of us, we know that it can't last forever. It leads to people feeling out of place, alone, and unworthy.

Out of place. . . .

Alone. . . .

Unworthy. . . .

It's a sad truth that those three descriptions fit the mold of how so many people across the millennial generation are feeling. It can hit anyone. It affects the people in the front of the class who know all the answers and have tons of friends the same way it does the person sitting at a lunch table all by themselves. Everyone is capable of feeling those things, and I am certainly no exception.

When I was going off to college I felt like I was leaving the entire world behind. I was moving away from the small town I had lived in my entire life to plant my stakes in a big city. I was scared. I was heading off to a place where I knew absolutely no one. I was going from being the big fish in a small pond to a single-cell bacterium in the Pacific Ocean.

Not that I was worried about making friends; I have always been the type of person who can talk to people. I am an off-the-charts extravert, and making friends had never been hard for me. It's just natural for me to go up to people I've never met and have a thirty-minute conversation with them about life. This drives my introverted wife crazy at times. It has just always been who I am. But that doesn't mean that I haven't experienced the feeling of extreme loneliness.

When I got to college I had some rough moments. I had a lot of friends. Or at least people who considered me a friend. Yet I always felt out of place for some reason. It seemed like it didn't matter if I was in a room full of people; I felt like I was unworthy of being there. I felt like everyone talked about me behind my back. I started believing that my friends were not my real friends, but only spent time with me because they felt bad for me. I felt anxious about reaching out to people to see if they wanted to get dinner or hang out because I feared that I would annoy them. I became consumed by the overwhelming feeling that nobody liked me. I started having panic attacks when I was in stressful situations. Moments like being on airplanes, going to the doctor, or sitting in big meetings. This was something I had never experienced before. Something that took me over a year to come out of. Something I didn't tell anyone about.

But it's funny how perception can change things in our lives. I had become so worried about moving to a big city and not knowing anybody, that I caused my fears to turn into my reality because of how often I dwelled on them. My friends weren't all out to get me and I didn't annoy them when I asked to hang out, but I sure did see it that way. Our perception of ourselves determines so much of how we act, feel, and live our lives. I saw myself as someone not-liked and unworthy of people's friendship, so I acted scared, lonely, and anxious. But when my perception of who I was went from being fixated on my own thoughts to being fixated on God's Word, my entire life turned around. I started turning back into the old Jake—a happy guy who loved making friends.

I am telling you this because I want people who are feeling this way to know that it can change. You can stop feeling anxious about people in your life and start feeling joyful because of the One that saved your life. Hold fast to that promise.

I love seeing people who hold fast to the promises of God. They live freely in who God says they are because they understand that He made them. These people are successful businessmen, janitors at the local elementary school, high school students, football coaches, and pretty much any other occupation or title you can think of. They are literally found anywhere and everywhere. They are from all different walks of life, but they are all similar in one way. They don't define themselves as a successful businessman, a janitor at the local elementary school, a high school student, or a football coach. No, instead, they look at themselves as loved sons and daughters of the King of the universe. They look at themselves as beloved creations of the Creator of everything. They find comfort in the consistency of their identity.

God doesn't want us to look at this world and define ourselves by things that we aren't. He wants us to look to Him in order to find the definition of who we are. We are all creations of an extraordinary Creator, and some of the greatest comfort can be found in that.

THE PRAYER

My biggest prayer is that each person reading this will come to see Jesus as a constant God. I pray that we all put down the variables in our lives that define us and shift our hearts toward Jesus so He can redefine us. He knows who we are. I pray that we all listen to what He says about us. After all, it will never change.

| | CH. 5 | |

BLAMELESS

When I was growing up as a little kid, I thought I was always one of the "good" kids. I would act up in school every once in a while, but for the most part I was among the right crowd of people. I listened to my parents and didn't cuss or lie for the majority of my younger years. I stayed out of major trouble and always made it home for dinner. I bathed every day and kept my room somewhat clean. At the time, I felt like I was an outstanding example of how a kid should be. However, that wasn't true.

Looking back on things now, I can see that I was really never one of the "good" kids. I might not have done stuff that was too terrible as a child, but I always wanted to. I seemed to be the friend who would always suggest the stupid ideas that

IMAGE

would likely end up getting everyone in trouble, and for some reason I was always able to convince people to do them with me. The worst part about it all was that I never seemed to learn from my mistakes. By the time I was in high school, things had escalated so much I began to do stuff I swore I never would.

I think that it is safe to say that I made a few questionable decisions when I was in high school. Actually, I think it's safe to say that the majority of my decisions in high school were questionable. I was always at the parties and always trying to talk to a different girl. I was also the only one of my friends with a fake ID at the age of 17, so I made plenty of risky liquor store runs across the tracks of my small town. I was that kid who clearly needed Jesus.

The majority of adults in my life viewed me as the kid who was really good at sports but never got into trouble. But people my age saw me as the kid who tried to sweet-talk his way out of being arrested with some of his buddies after getting caught toilet-papering 14 houses in one night. (It worked.) I was seen as a dumb jock, a womanizer, a party animal, and a "typical high school football player." And I lived up to those labels perfectly.

Honestly, I never minded being called those things. In my mind it was an honor be a typical football player, and I enjoyed partying. I didn't really care that I was awarded the "biggest flirt" as my senior superlative in the yearbook. I didn't even care that some girls hated me because of how much of a jerk I was. I mean, how could I argue with any of them? It was completely reasonable that people viewed me how they did.

The majority of people I knew who were believers in Jesus never seemed to talk to me about Him. They must have viewed me as a lost cause. They probably thought I was too far gone to be brought back. I mean, I didn't blame them; I thought that too. It wasn't until the week of my high school graduation that I realized just how destructive my lifestyle was. I'm not sure what made me come to that realization. It could've been the two different girls that slapped me in the face in a span of 15 seconds. Or it could have been the fact that I got belligerently drunk on a Tuesday night when I had to go to school the next day. All I knew was that the Lord spoke into my heart that week and convicted me in a way that I had never experienced before.

I had tons of questions about what was going on in my heart during this time. I knew that what I was feeling wasn't from me, so I called up one of my best friends at the time. She loved Jesus, and is still one of the greatest people I know. Her name is Garrett. She was one of the only people who never gave up on me in high school. She walked through all of senior year with me and witnessed me at my worst, but she kept trying her hardest to point me back to Jesus. Because of her faithfulness, I decided to ask her to go to Chick-fil-A with me so I could ask her some questions.

I really had no idea how to start the conversation that was about to go down at a booth inside the Dwarf House. I was nervous. I had never really tried to bring up anything like this to any of my friends in such a serious way. I had always considered myself a Christian, but I had a feeling that after this conversation with Garrett I would find out that I was more of a cultural Christian than anything else.

I can't exactly remember how the conversation went, but I know that it changed my life forever. At some point during that 45-minute time period, the Holy Spirit took hold of my heart and I was never going to be the same again. Garrett told me that she had prayed for me constantly throughout the last year. She said that she saw great potential for me to be used for the advancement of God's Kingdom. Nobody had told me that since I was a little kid. I believe that the Lord used Garrett to change my heart forever.

After we met at CFA I decided I was going to start going to a summer Bible study with a few of my friends from Young Life. That summer Bible study changed the trajectory of my life in a way I never thought was possible. By the end of those three months walking through the book of Romans, it was crystal clear to me that I was being called to a life of full-time ministry. The following months after that were some of the most amazing, challenging, and extraordinary months I have ever experienced. I knew that my life was going to completely revolve around Jesus and ministering to people. I was excited about doing so, and I could feel the Lord placing that on my heart more and more each day. But one thing also stayed with me—my past.

THE PAST IS YOUR PLATFORM

During the next several months after I decided to follow Jesus I had some real struggles with my past. I knew everything that I had done. I couldn't hide it from myself. I couldn't escape it. I couldn't forget all of the nights that I fooled around with girls or drank way too much. I couldn't forget the moments when I blatantly lied just because I could. And the worst one was that I couldn't forget all the people I had hurt. It was like this dark cloud rained over me wherever I went, and even though I felt so compelled to minister to people, I felt like I had no right to because of my past. I thought that my past made it impossible for me to have a future completely devoted to Jesus.

I'm sure that some of you have been in this situation before. We have all done something bad, and I'm sure we all have a season in our life that we look back on and regret. We think of all of the things we did wrong before we started following Jesus and the enemy begins to tell us that we aren't good enough to help advance the gospel. He whispers in our ear to remind us of all of the terrible things we did in the past so it seems like we can never escape them. If you're anything like me then you probably beat yourself up over this. I can remember all the moments when I would stay up at night and wonder how I could ever talk to a high school guy about purity when I was the poster child for the un-pure when I was his age. It was totally affecting my entire life, and eventually I began to identify myself, and my ministry, by my past. I would only have the conversations that I felt I was worthy of having. I would stay away from telling people not to have sex or drink underage because I let the enemy convince me that I had no right to tell them that. I saw myself as a screw-up who had to work his butt off in order to wipe away his past. I was always trying to do whatever I could to cancel out my sins. Needless to say, it was the most exhausting time in my entire life.

I let the enemy completely infiltrate my thought life until I started believing the lies that he was feeding me.

"You will never help advance the gospel . . . just look at what you used to do."

"How can you believe that you can even say the name Jesus; you don't deserve to even pick up your Bible."

"Your wife will never fully love you because of all that you've done."

I don't know if any of you have ever experienced that before, but trust me when I say that it's terrible. I knew that I needed to fight these thoughts, but I couldn't help thinking about them. Then one day the Lord spoke to me in such a clear way.

I can remember sitting in my apartment in Kennesaw, Georgia, one morning drinking coffee. I had just finished reading Scripture and I was praying over my day. The Lord laid something on my heart that morning that changed my life forever. I was praying about my past and how I wished I could just forget it. I was asking Him to banish it from my thoughts and for strength to help my mind not stray to certain things. That's when the Lord did something incredible. I felt Him telling me that He didn't bring me out of my darkest moments so I would look like I had never done anything wrong. He was telling me to use my past as a platform to be able to tell people how far He had brought me. He was telling me to use it as a testimony of His grace and redemption to assure people that He could do the same for them.

Up until this point it was clear that Satan was the only one I was letting use my past. I was trying to hide my past from God, even though He already knew about it anyway. It was the perfect time for God to do one of the things that only He can do. When He broke through the wall I had constructed, that I thought was protecting the world from my past, I realized that He doesn't want us to hide the dark parts of our stories. He wants us to use them as leverage in a world that feels like it can't relate to Christians.

This revelation showed me that I wasn't unworthy to speak to high school guys about sex and drinking. I was actually the perfect candidate for it. I could look them in the eyes, and being completely honest, tell them about a life that is so much greater than any teenage temptation. I could tell them that if God was willing to save me, then He would definitely be willing to save them. Nobody is too far gone that they can't be brought back.

OVERFLOWING HOLINESS

I never expected the Lord to be able to do such amazing things through my testimony. I have seen people's lives completely transformed through the transparency of how He has lead me to tell my story. I'm sure that many of you have been—or still are—in the same situation I was in. You feel broken, useless, guilty, shameful, and disgusted. I'm sure that many of you keep things from your past buried deep inside of you because you fear that if anyone found out about them they would never want to talk to you again. I know how that feels.

Our past sins have the ability to define and cripple us in a way that makes it extremely hard to proclaim the gospel. But that's only if we let them. Because the gospel has the ability to define us and enhance our ability to share the love, grace, and hope found in Jesus. When I started writing this book, I got together with some of my closest friends and we started walking through some of the ideas presented throughout these pages. We talked about how people let their past define them, and we explored what Scripture says about that. This one verse in Ephesians 1 completely wrecked our hearts when we read it:

> *Even as he [the Father] chose us in him [Jesus] before the foundation of the world, that we should be holy and blameless before him.* (Ephesians 1:4, ESV)

That verse can be a game-changer in our lives if we let it. The thought that we, as believers in Jesus, are holy and blameless in the sight of God is something that a lot of us never think about. So as Christians, we should never allow the enemy to grab hold of our thought life and let our past sins define us. We are holy in the sight of God. We aren't perfect, but we are forgiven. We are blameless.

What makes this so incredible is the fact that we can't make ourselves holy and blameless. Every one of us has sinned and there is no way we can go through our whole life without sinning. We can never earn the title of being holy and blameless. There is no good deed that we could do to be considered blameless in the sight of God. We can't become holy because of a really good week we had where we barely sinned. This identity we have does not come from anything we could do. It comes from everything that Jesus has done.

Jesus lived a life of overflowing holiness. He was completely sinless and righteous in every way possible. He was completely blameless. Isn't it awesome that He's willing to share that title with us? After we come to know Jesus He lavishes us with new life. The new life He gives us is one where we are completely and utterly blameless in the sight of God. Jesus' holiness washes over our lives and God no longer sees us as who we were, but He sees us as what we have become—holy and blameless.

This proves that we are not blameless because of anything we did, but we are blameless because of everything Jesus did. My favorite way I have ever heard it described is that it isn't performance-based holiness but positionally based holiness. We are holy and blameless because of where we are in Christ.

This truth is such a game-changer because it kills the idea that our past can hold us back. We should no longer feel guilt or shame because of the sins we have committed. Guilt and shame are not from the Lord, but from the enemy. The truth allows us to ditch the false identity so many of us have put on our lives that says we are not good enough to be loved by Jesus. It allows us to enter into a new mindset of saying, "I know I have sinned, but that's not holding me back. I am holy and blameless in the sight of God. Not because of anything I have done, but because of everything Jesus did. Therefore, I am going to live my life in complete and utter freedom knowing that my sins do not define me, but my Savior defines me, and He calls me holy and blameless."

FEARLESSLY PROPELLED

The truth of the matter is that there is no surprising God. He knows everything before it even happens. He knew that you and your girlfriend were going to mess up. He knew that you were going to lie to your parents. He knew that you were going to say some things to your best friend that you really shouldn't have. He knew about all of that stuff before you were even born. He's omniscient and all-powerful. There is nothing that gets past Him.

If you're anything like me, then the fact that nothing gets past God should scare you a little bit. However, at the same time it should comfort you. Why? Because yes, Jesus knew you were going to sin before you were born, but He also knew you were going to sin when He was being questioned by Pilate in the governor's headquarters. He knew about all of your sin after they released Barabbas and the whole crowd yelled for Jesus' crucifixion. Jesus knew about your sin when they were driving those nails into His hands and feet. And guess what? He was still completely willing to die on that cross so that you can live a life that isn't defined by your mistakes.

Jesus didn't die on the cross so that we could be timid and held back by our past. He died so that we could be fearless and propelled forward because our past is wiped clean. If you ever feel like your sins are too big to be forgiven, then you should visit the life of Paul. In 1 Timothy, Paul writes:

Here is a trustworthy saying that deserves full acceptance: Christ Jesus came into the world to save sinners—of whom I am the worst. But for that very reason I was shown mercy so that in me, the worst of sinners, Christ Jesus might display his immense patience as an example for

Jesus didn't die on the cross

 so that we could be timid

and held back by our past.

He died

so that we could be fearless

and propelled forward

because our past

is wiped clean.

those who would believe in him and receive eternal life. (1 Timothy 1:15–16, NIV)

I know what some of you may be thinking. You're probably wondering how a man who wrote a huge portion of the New Testament could consider himself the worst of all sinners. Well, before Paul became the most well-known Christian missionary of all time, he was a Jewish man on a different type of mission. Paul absolutely hated Christians. He publicly announced that he despised Jesus and thought he was a fake, blasphemous piece of garbage. He would hunt down Christians and do everything in his power to prosecute them.

Paul was a murderer of those who loved Jesus. He wanted them all dead and wanted the name of Jesus to be eradicated from the face of the Earth. He was public enemy number one against the church. That is, until he had a very real encounter with Jesus one day while he was on his way to Damascus. And that encounter with Jesus shaped the remainder of Paul's life (Acts 9). He stopped trying to kill Christians and instead started leading them. He went from being a murderer to a missionary all because of one encounter with Jesus. All of this was possible because Paul understood that the people he had harmed and the sins he had committed did not define him. He understood that Jesus defined him. He realized that he had become holy and blameless. He understood this so much so, that he was the one who wrote Ephesians 1:4 that tells us we are holy and blameless.

Paul is also seen throughout Scripture talking about his past. He is candid about how he persecuted the church, and we just saw where he admitted to being the worst of all sinners. Paul is a perfect example of how God calls us to use our past as a platform to stand on and preach Jesus' message of grace.

THE PRAYER

I pray that you realize God can use anybody's story to bring Himself glory. You are never too far gone to be used by Him, and if you are in Christ there is nothing you can do that would be able to shape your core identity away from what He says it is. I pray that we all stop living crippled by our past mistakes, but instead live powerfully in God's forgiveness.

Ephesians 1:4 has radically altered my life and how I view myself. It allows me to live with freedom in the fact that Jesus sees me as holy and blameless. It has softened my heart to forgive others, as well. I know that if Jesus can forgive me for all that I have done, there is no way that I shouldn't be able to forgive other people for what they have done. This has helped me mend broken relationships that were in my life and hash out some things with people that I have been upset about for years.

I pray that God works within you in a very similar way and you're able to mend some broken relationships in your own life.

The fact that God views me as holy and blameless allows me to speak boldly about what He has done in my life. I pray that for some of you, it gives you the nudge that you need in order to fully accept Jesus into your life and become holy and blameless as well. And for others of you, I pray that you realize that because you have already accepted Jesus, the words "holy" and "blameless" are written across your core identity.

| | CH. 6 | |

ALIVE

Growing up I had a great-grandmother who was consistently in my life. She was old and had severe Alzheimer's disease, but I still saw her at least once a week when I was a kid. She lived with my dad's mom, who was her daughter, and I would go over to their house all the time. I can remember all of the instances she would play hide and seek with me and my siblings and then forget what she was doing and go watch TV in the middle of the game. Her mind was in bad shape. It eventually got so bad that we had to check her into a nursing home.

When I was still a kid she would have moments of clarity. There would be about a five-minute span every once in a while where she knew exactly who I was and was completely fine. But as she got older, the disease got worse and she eventually could hardly talk. She passed away when I was 19 years old at the age of 93. My grandmother asked me if I would preach at her funeral. I remember being nervous about taking on such a daunting task. Not because I was afraid of public speaking, but because I had never spoken at a funeral before.

Funeral homes and gravesites are places where people are usually sad. They are synonymous with death, so it makes sense. That was hard for me. When I speak at places I'm usually bringing good news. I'm usually speaking with joy and talking about Jesus. I'm usually happy and excited about what I'm going to say. I was stumped on how to prepare for a funeral. I didn't know how to speak to a crowd of people who were going through one of the hardest times in their lives.

I dwelled on this for a couple of days, and I became more and more nervous about what I was going to say. On the morning of the funeral I still hadn't prepared anything and that's when I started to get really nervous. So I sat down at my kitchen table and I began to pray. I just started talking to God and asking Him how I should go about handling this sensitive time in my family's life. Then He revealed something awesome to me. He put the fact on my heart that my great-grandmother had loved Jesus more than anyone, or anything, else. That's when my eyes were opened to what I was going to talk about. I started jotting down my notes and my nervousness quickly turned into excitement.

When the funeral started there were several people crying in the crowd. Most were close family members of mine and others were old friends. I could see on their face that they were destroyed over the fact that we had all lost someone we loved so much. I caught eyes with my big brother and then walked to the podium and opened up the service with a prayer.

The very first thing I said to my grieving family was that this was a very sad moment wrapped up within a very joyous reality. Most of their faces turned up at me and I could tell some were confused. I saw my mom and dad start smiling and I knew that they understood. I went on to talk about how my great-grandmother's life didn't end here. Her body might have worn out and been laid to rest, but her spirit was more alive than ever.

You see, my great-grandmother loved Jesus. She knew Jesus on a personal level and had been made alive through Him. She was holy, blameless, pure, and alive. Because of this, her funeral was not meant to be a sad occasion. Her funeral was meant to be a celebration of Jesus and of her life on Earth. So that's what we did. As I started talking I unraveled how we were inside of a joyous reality. We smiled and laughed and cried and told stories. We knew that our great-grandmother was not dead. We knew that she was in the best place she could ever be, so we spoke with excitement about her life instead of with sorrow about her death.

That's what is so beautiful about the gospel. It allows for a small-town, country family like mine to celebrate the life of a 93-year-old woman who will never be dead. Jesus came into this world to defeat death, and that's exactly what He did. However, He didn't just defeat death for Himself, but He also defeated it for all of us. He paved the way for us to have the opportunity to live forever.

REAL LIFE

The story of Jesus is the most significant thing to ever happen on Earth. It was a game-changing moment in history, and it continues to be a game-changing moment in millions of people's lives today, including mine. There has never been anything that has come close to the magnitude of Jesus' story, and there never will be. His life will forever remain the most extraordinary story of love, grace, and redemption the Earth has ever known.

I think one of the biggest problems with modern-day Christianity is that we fail to see Jesus' life on Earth as something that actually happened. We say we believe it, but we view it as just an old wives' tale that teaches good moral behavior. I want to actually take a look at the last moments of Jesus' life on Earth before He was crucified. But while you read it, I challenge you to view it as what it was: an actual moment in history. Don't treat it as a story you heard as a kid. Look at it with fresh perspective, and view the cross as a moment in time instead of a story in a book.

For those of you who don't know the backstory behind the life and crucifixion of Jesus, please allow me to explain for a moment. For hundreds and hundreds of years the Jewish people during biblical times had been promised a savior by God. He was going to be the answer to their prayers and the deliverer of their salvation. You see, the Old Testament deal was all about performance. The people of that time had to live their life in a certain way that pleased God, and they had to offer animal sacrifices to Him regularly in order for their sins to be forgiven. The only way to enter into the kingdom of heaven was to live a righteous life. As you can imagine, this was extremely hard. They were told that they couldn't sin and if they did they had to make a blood sacrifice to have their sin washed away. It was a tiring and tedious way of life.

I'm a firm believer that one of the coolest parts of the Ten Commandments is that they show us that nobody can follow a simple list of ten rules. They show us that we need someone who can to enter into our lives and save us. That's where Jesus comes in. Jesus had to live a perfect life on Earth that was completely free of sin in order to be our savior, and that's exactly what he did. He would live a perfect life and then be killed for the atonement of all people. It would be one final sacrifice for the sins of the world. Jesus was going to take the place of all of the animals that were sacrificed for the redemption of sin once and for all. He would die innocent, perfect, and holy, so that the rest of the world might be saved. The weight of everyone's sin and shame would fall on Jesus in a moment in time where heaven and Earth collide, and history would be changed forever.

The Old Testament texts show us that the very people Jesus came to do this for would be the ones who ended up killing Him. It shows us that the people who had been waiting years for Him to come onto the scene would deny Him to His face. So this savior entered into the picture, lived a perfect, sinless, righteous life, and was murdered because people didn't believe He was the one they'd been waiting for. They thought He was crazy when He told them that He was going to rise up from the dead after three days. All of the religious leaders at the time hated Him. They wanted Him dead. So they made it happen. Here is what happened when they finally arrested Him:

> *The soldiers assigned to the governor took Jesus into the governor's palace and got the entire*

brigade together for some fun. They stripped him and dressed him in a red toga. They plaited a crown from branches of a thornbush and set it on his head. They put a stick in his right hand for a scepter. Then they knelt before him in mocking reverence: "Bravo, King of the Jews!" they said. "Bravo!" Then they spit on him and hit him on the head with the stick. When they had had their fun, they took off the toga and put his own clothes back on him. Then they proceeded out to the crucifixion.

Along the way they came on a man from Cyrene named Simon and made him carry Jesus' cross. Arriving at Golgotha, the place they call "Skull Hill," they offered him a mild painkiller (a mixture of wine and myrrh), but when he tasted it he wouldn't drink it.

After they had finished nailing him to the cross and were waiting for him to die, they whiled away the time by throwing dice for his clothes. Above his head they had posted the criminal charge against him: THIS IS JESUS, THE KING OF THE JEWS. Along with him, they also crucified two criminals, one to his right, the other to his left. People passing along the road jeered, shaking their heads in mock lament: "You bragged that you could tear down the Temple and then rebuild it in three days—so show us your stuff! Save yourself! If you're really God's Son, come down from that cross!"

The high priests, along with the religion scholars and leaders, were right there mixing it up with the rest of them, having a great time poking fun at him: "He saved others—he can't save himself! King of Israel, is he? Then let him get down from that cross. We'll all become believers then! He was so sure of God—well, let him rescue his 'Son' now—if he wants him! He did claim to be God's Son, didn't he?" Even the two criminals crucified next to him joined in the mockery.

From noon to three, the whole earth was dark. Around midafternoon Jesus groaned out of the depths, crying loudly, "Eli, Eli, lama sabachthani?" which means, "My God, my God, why have you abandoned me?"

Some bystanders who heard him said, "He's calling for Elijah." One of them ran and got a sponge soaked in sour wine and lifted it on a stick so he could drink. The others joked, "Don't be in such a hurry. Let's see if Elijah comes and saves him."

But Jesus, again crying out loudly, breathed his last.

At that moment, the Temple curtain was ripped in two, top to bottom. There was an earthquake, and rocks were split in pieces. What's more, tombs were opened up, and many bodies of believers asleep in their graves were raised. (After Jesus' resurrection, they left the tombs, entered the holy city, and appeared to many.)

The captain of the guard and those with him, when they saw the earthquake and everything else that was happening, were scared to death. They said, "This has to be the Son of God!"

There were also quite a few women watching from a distance, women who had followed Jesus from Galilee in order to serve him. Among them were Mary Magdalene, Mary the mother of James and Joseph, and the mother of the Zebedee brothers.

Late in the afternoon a wealthy man from Arimathea, a disciple of Jesus, arrived. His name was Joseph. He went to Pilate and asked for Jesus' body. Pilate granted his request. Joseph took the body and wrapped it in clean linens, put it in his own tomb, a new tomb only recently cut into the rock, and rolled a large stone across the entrance. Then he went off. But Mary Magdalene and the other Mary stayed, sitting in plain view of the tomb.

After sundown, the high priests and Pharisees arranged a meeting with Pilate. They said, "Sir, we just remembered that that liar an-

nounced while he was still alive, 'After three days I will be raised.' We've got to get that tomb sealed until the third day. There's a good chance his disciples will come and steal the corpse and then go around saying, 'He's risen from the dead.' Then we'll be worse off than before, the final deceit surpassing the first."

Pilate told them, "You will have a guard. Go ahead and secure it the best you can." So they went out and secured the tomb, sealing the stone and posting guards.
(Matthew 27:27–66, MSG)

That actually happened. It's not some made-up story meant to make people feel bad. The cross was an actual moment in history. The Temple curtain really did rip from top to bottom. The soldiers really did become frozen with fear while the earthquake really was happening. Believers who were dead really did come back to life. People actually spat on Jesus while they were mocking him, and he really was nailed to a tree. It was brutal. It was terrifying. It was the darkest moment in all of humanity. Why? Because the savior of humanity was dead.

But hallelujah, what a savior He is because the story does not end there. Out of the darkest moment in all of history comes the most beautiful moment in all of history. Matthew 28 picks up right where we left off.

But hallelujah,

what a savior He is

because the story

does not end there.

Out of the darkest moment

in all of history

comes

the most beautiful moment

in all of history.

After the Sabbath, as the first light of the new week dawned, Mary Magdalene and the other Mary came to keep vigil at the tomb. Suddenly the earth reeled and rocked under their feet as God's angel came down from heaven, came right up to where they were standing. He rolled back the stone and then sat on it. Shafts of lightning blazed from him. His garments shimmered snow-white. The guards at the tomb were scared to death. They were so frightened, they couldn't move.

The angel spoke to the women: "There is nothing to fear here. I know you're looking for Jesus, the One they nailed to the cross. He is not here. He was raised, just as he said. Come and look at the place where he was placed.

"Now, get on your way quickly and tell his disciples, 'He is risen from the dead. He is going on ahead of you to Galilee. You will see him there.' That's the message."
(Matthew 28:1–7, MSG)

Jesus came into this world to be the ultimate sacrifice for sins. He knew He was going to die a terrible death, and He knew He would be mocked, tortured, and hated by many. But He also knew He wouldn't stay dead. He knew He was going to defeat death, sin, and the grave. He knew that you would be worth everything He had to endure in order to make that happen. The curse of sin is a terrible, terrible thing. Scripture tells us that the wages of sin is death (Romans 6:23), and I think Louie Giglio said it best when he said, "Sin doesn't make us bad; sin makes us dead." And since we are all born into sin, that means that we are all born spiritually dead and in need of a savior.

The fact that sin makes us dead is the reason we need Jesus. He was the final sacrifice for sins, which means that He has the power to wash sins away. Consequently, if He washes all of our sins away, then He also washes away the wages of sin, which is death. And the great thing is that all we have to do is believe in Him. By believing that Jesus was nailed to a cross and died, then descended into hell in which He defeated death, and rose victorious over the grave on the third day, we are washed of the condition that sin leaves us in. Therefore, if we acknowledge that Jesus is our Lord and Savior, then we will no longer be dead. Instead we will be able to experience the wonders of being alive in Christ.

But all of this is predicated on the second chunk of Scripture from Matthew 28. If Jesus' story ended at the cross, then there would be no Christian faith. If He never rose from the grave, never showing the world that death has no control over Him, then we would still have to slaughter lambs and try to live a perfect life in order for our sins to be forgiven. But because Jesus is alive, I am alive. Because He is who He is, I am who I am.

COUNTERING THE CONDITION

It's interesting how we don't realize our condition of sin when we are spiritually dead. We just live life and have no recognition of the fact that we are trapped in a lifeless body. It's not until we come to know Jesus that we are able to look back on our previous condition and see the trouble we were in. When we experience true life, we realize how empty the alternative is.

God realizes the condition that sin leaves us in from the beginning. He is never blind to the fact that we are dead without Him. He longs to bring us into His family, which is why Jesus was willing to go through the worst kind of torture imaginable. It's His great love that causes light to shine out of darkness, and it's by grace that He offers us life to the full.

> *But God, being rich in mercy, because of the great love with which he loved us, even when we were dead in our trespasses, made us alive together with Christ—by grace you have been saved.* (Ephesians 2:4–5, ESV)

Because God is rich in mercy and full of love, we are alive. We have received that identity from Him strictly because of who He is. There is no other person, friend group, or success that could give us that label. Only God. Because only the person of Jesus is capable of countering the condition of sin.

Jesus' story is the reason I spoke with excitement and joy at my grandmother's funeral. Because she wasn't dead, and hadn't been dead for a very long time. But when she was still dead in her sin, Jesus died on the cross for her, and for you, and for me. She knew that was true. I know that is true, and many of my friends know that is true. I'm so blessed to be able to look at the Jake that was dead in his sins and rejoice in the fact that I'm no longer there.

This gift of life that Jesus is giving isn't just for the "good people." It's for literally everyone. It's for the murderers and the thieves just as much as it is for the people that go to church every Sunday. How can this be? It's because God is rich in mercy and He has great love for us all. He doesn't want any of us to remain dead in our sins, but He wants us all to become alive through Christ.

DEATH TO LIFE

Being able to experience people coming from death to life through Jesus is my favorite part of life. It's the reason I became involved in ministry and started working with Young Life in college. Being able to witness people finally grasp what the story of Jesus' life means for them is something that I would not trade for anything else in this world.

Just two weeks prior to writing this chapter I got to experience it with one of my Young Life guys.

I was sitting with the middle school group I lead when one of my guys asked a question that he said he had always wondered about.

"When did Jesus die the second time?"

This is one of those questions that you don't really expect from kids who grew up going to church, but I could tell he was genuinely curious. It was one of those cases where this seventh-grade guy had "prayed a prayer" when he was eight, but never actually knew what he was praying. This happens all the time in churches, especially in the South. However, I just explained to him the reality of the life of Jesus as if he had never heard it before. I explained to him one of my favorite things to explain to people: Jesus never died a second time. Jesus is still alive.

He was a little confused by that answer, so I went into more detail in order to explain it to him. We talked about how if Jesus never rose from the grave, then the Christian faith would not exist. Also, if Jesus died again after He rose from the grave, then the Christian faith would not exist. The Christian faith is based on the fact that we believe Jesus is still alive. We believe the Scriptures when they say that He ascended into heaven instead of being buried in the ground for good (Acts 1:9). We believe that He conquered death. Not just for three days, but forever. We believe that because Jesus is alive, we have the same opportunity to be alive.

Through this conversation this guy finally started realizing that the Christian faith is different. He finally understood that it is the only faith in the world that worships a God who is alive. I could see him begin to process everything I had said, and his facial expressions showed that he was thinking pretty hard. He apparently processed this for the next 24 hours until the next night when we were all gathered together again. That night he told us that he had decided to accept Jesus completely. He was finally able to grasp the magnitude, yet simplicity, of the gospel. He was dead and in need of a savior, and Jesus is alive and able to save him.

Being alive should give us the most freedom we have ever known. We shouldn't be afraid to take chances in life for something that we believe in. We shouldn't be afraid to talk about Jesus to people who don't know him. We shouldn't be afraid to die, because after this life on Earth, we're going to a place so wonderful we can't even begin to fathom its beauty.

So as a Christian, never again do you have to worry about not being the prettiest girl in your sorority. Why not? Because you're alive. As a Christian you don't need to stress over one bad grade, because you will never experience the feeling of eternal separation from God. And as a

Christian, being the best athlete in school for only your glory is a microscopic factor in life when you look at how you miraculously went from death to life.

THE PRAYER

I pray that through reading this chapter, you realize who you are if you know Jesus: completely alive. I pray that this turns the tables for people who believe in Jesus, but are still living trapped by the fear of death. I hope these words have influenced you in a similar way that they have me, and you're able to live in the freedom that comes from the life of Jesus.

I pray that someone who isn't a Christian reads this. I hope that you understand that you too can be alive through Christ. I pray that the Lord speaks to you in a way that you have never experienced, and that when He does, you will begin your new journey of full, extraordinary life.

| | CH. 7 | |

CHILDREN

One of my favorite things about growing up was the fact that my parents were both in education. My mom was my fifth grade teacher and my dad was my principal two different times. He was with me in elementary school, and again all four years of high school. Most people would come up and ask me if I hated having my dad as my high school principal, but I actually loved it.

Conversations about having my dad as principal went one of two ways. People either said, "Dang, man. That must suck. You don't get a break at all." The other response I would get went a little bit differently. People would say, "Dude, you're so lucky. I bet you get away with everything, huh?"

I guess the best answer to each of these questions is just a simple "yes." I would get in trouble with my dad at home and then he would often still be mad at me the next day at school. So it was hard at times because I would have the pressure of not only trying to please the principal, but also my parent. There were certain teachers who were a lot harder on me than they were on other students because they didn't want to show any favoritism to their boss's kid. It was like they used me as a power play to show the other kids in the class that they were the real deal. If they were hard on the principal's kid, then they would definitely be hard on everyone else.

But at the same time, I also had things a lot easier. If I ever forgot to get a paper signed I would just go to Mrs. Chrystal's office (my dad's secretary and a very close family friend), and she would use a stamp with his signature on it to sign my papers. I was also allowed to go get things from my car during the day, or even run home if I left something I needed for school. There were even times when I was able to be late for class because I got caught up talking about football, hunting, or fishing with my dad. I was written a free late pass every time.

Even though I had a lot of benefits from my dad being my principal, I still struggled with it at times. I had to live my life differently than the other kids because everyone in town knew my dad. In school I had to be on my best behavior because my dad was just right down the hall. There were certain things I couldn't talk about or say and certain things that I was required to do because of who my dad was. It was clear that I had to live my life by a different code than the other kids in school. But even though I had to live differently I still believed the good outweighed the bad, and I absolutely loved having my dad as my principal. I loved my dad and I was proud to be his son. And sure, I messed up a lot. There were countless times where I strayed from the life I was supposed to live and did something stupid, but my dad never hung that over my head. He would always talk to me about it, forgive me for it, and keep loving the crap out of me. My mess-ups never changed the fact that he was still my dad, and I was still his son.

Even though there were clear times in which my dad had to play the role of the principal towards me, he always put his role as my dad first. He would choose me over his job any day, but I think that was an extremely fine line he had to walk at times. But no matter which side of the line he chose to step on, I knew that at the end of the day it wasn't going to change the fact that he was my dad.

My dad and I are now in two totally different stages of life. I'm no longer a student and instead I work in ministry. He has retired from the public school system and doesn't ever go to the old high school anymore. Even though our lives are completely different, one thing remains the same: I am his son and he is my dad. I say all of this to remind us all that, as Christians, one thing will always remain the same: we will be God's children and he will be our Father.

A NEW FAMILY

Family is one of the most important things to me. The culture in my family is one that I wouldn't trade for anything. During my childhood, we would have family dinners at least once a week. Now when I say family dinners, I don't mean just me, my parents, and my brother and sister—we had that type of family dinner every night. I'm talking about grandparents, aunts and uncles, cousins, nieces and nephews, and even great-aunts! We had an extremely close relationship with the whole family.

Memories that came from those family dinners are memories I'll cherish for the rest of my life. My family is definitely one of a kind, but they're not my only family. They're my earthly family. Scripture tells us that after we accept Jesus, we enter in to a divine family with every other person who has come from death to life in Jesus. And the Head of this family is God Almighty Himself.

For those who are led by the Spirit of God are the children of God. The Spirit you received does not make you slaves, so that you live in fear again; rather, the Spirit you received brought about your adoption to sonship. And by Him we cry, "Abba, Father." The Spirit himself testifies with our Spirit that we are God's children. Now if we are children, then we are heirs—heirs of God and co-heirs with Christ, if indeed we share in his sufferings in order that we may also share in his glory. (Romans 8:14–17, NIV)

I think being the principal's kid is pretty cool, but being God's children? That's on a level all its own. We aren't talking about some made-up god that's in some random book that was written thousands of years ago. We are talking about a God who breathed His book into existence through His Spirit and who created everything you can ever think of or imagine. He created the seas and at any moment He could drink them dry and leave the whole Earth barren. He created the mountains and if He ever wanted to He could just press His thumb down on them and they would go flat. We are talking about a God that is big enough to swallow a solar system, yet cares enough to intricately design the process of what happens inside of a caterpillar's cocoon.

This God we are talking about is so great it isn't even possible for us to understand Him fully. He is so great we can't even make sense of some of

His characteristics. This God is so great that people look death in the eye every day and they aren't afraid because they know that the God we are talking about is on their side. And just think: we are called His children. Every person who has ever called on the name of Jesus and has been brought from death to life through Him immediately enters into a divine family with God as their Father.

NO LONGER SLAVES

I love how in Romans 8:15 it talks about how the Spirit we received from God frees us from being slaves to fear. It makes me think of all the stories I've heard over the years about people being little and being bullied by an older kid. They always start out talking about how they were afraid to get anywhere near the kid who picked on them because they didn't want to get hurt. They hated going to school, or to the park, or anywhere public that the bully might be. They were consumed by this fear of getting made fun of or beat up by someone that they couldn't handle by themselves. And then, more times than not, I'd hear about how their dad would find out. Somehow, word would get back to their dad that his son or daughter was getting bullied, and that was never okay with him. So as the story would unfold, they would talk about how the next time they went to the park their dad would always join along.

We are talking about a God

that is big enough

to swallow a solar system,

yet cares enough

to intricately design

the process of what happens

inside a caterpillar's cocoon.

Where the stories go from here has always been my favorite part. They would go on to tell me about how their dad talked to the "little punk bully" and towered over him in dominance. They always talk about how safe they felt in that moment. They knew that their dad had their back and that he was so much bigger than any schoolyard bully. Isn't that a great example of how we can view our father-child relationship with God? Although God might never go to someone and scare-talk them into not messing with you, He will always show up and be right by your side. So just think of how great you felt when your dad was there to save you from things as a kid, and then multiply that level of freedom times infinity. Because the Heavenly Father who is telling you that you're no longer a slave to fear isn't just talking about some schoolyard bully. He's talking about no longer being afraid of death. No longer being afraid of the demons that are in your life. He's talking about things that are huge but not huge enough. Because the Spirit you receive from God after going from death to life in Jesus casts out fear of even the biggest things.

GOOD, GOOD FATHER

The fact that I can say that I am a child of God is so incredible to me. There are times when I'm listening to the worship song "Good Good Father" by Pat Barrett, and I just break out in tears. However, there are also times when I listen to a sermon or read in Scripture about how I am a child of God and I don't even seem to care. It's almost as if I have heard it so many times that I have become numb to what it means. It's like it has become a modern-day Christian security blanket that we pull out during hard times. If someone is struggling with life we just look at them and say, "Hey. You're a child of God. It will all be okay." That's totally true. If they are a Christian, then they are a child of God, and in the long run it will be okay! But why is that something we tend to only use as a "get well soon" card?

The fact that we as Christians are children of God is something that we should hold on to every second of every day. We should wake up in the morning and thank God for adopting us as sons and daughters. We should live our lives in such a unique and incredible way that everyone who comes in contact with us knows we are different. We should live them in a way that could only be possible if God was our Father. There is no way we should remain numb to the fact that we are children of God. It is literally who we are. It is one of the core characteristics of our identity.

The song I mentioned earlier, "Good Good Father," has a chorus that relates so much to what we are talking about right now. It goes:

> You're a good good Father, it's who You are
> It's who You are, it's who You are
> And I'm loved by You, it's who I am
> It's who I am, it's who I am

I feel like that sums it up perfectly. He is a good, good Father, and because of that, we are loved by Him. That's who He is, and who He is makes us who we are—loved sons and daughters.

I get so upset when I see someone who is torn down by life and their failures. Their career didn't work out the way they expected it to or they didn't end up with the grades they wanted. They label themselves as failures. They define themselves as people who weren't quite good enough. That absolutely breaks my heart. I feel for those people, because I used to define myself in that way. I have been in that boat. I've experienced life when I felt like I had nothing to offer because I didn't meet the expectations of myself or of others. I hate that we can fall into that trap so easily.

I want people to know who they are. I want them to know that they aren't failures, even if they haven't been "successful" recently. I want them to know that other people's expectations don't matter and they can't possibly please everyone. I just want them to know that God made them individually, and specifically, and uniquely. They have the opportunity to have a part of their core identity be a "child of the king of the universe."

Let's look at the ideal father-child relationship. A father cares for his child in a variety of different ways. He is the protector. He makes sure that harm doesn't come near his kids. He provides financially for his children. He is the leader of the family and tends to be the wisest one with advice about life. His kids think he is superman when they're little, and sometimes even after they grow up. The father in the family is usually strong, loving, caring, and smart. But let's be honest. That's not the norm for a vast amount of people in this world.

I'm not blind to the fact that some fathers suck. Some fathers leave their kids before they're even born because they don't want to deal with the responsibilities of raising a child. Some fathers can't protect their children from harm because they are the ones causing the harm. Some steal from their family instead of supporting their family. There are fathers out there who couldn't care less about their children.

The fact of the matter is that all earthly fathers are going to mess up at times. Some might mess up all the time, and some might do it very rarely, but nonetheless they will still all mess up. I have no way of knowing which end of the spectrum your father might fall on, but I know one thing about every one of you. You are either a Christian and have a relationship with a Heavenly Father who is perfect, or you are not a Christian and you have the opportunity to have a relationship with a Heavenly Father who is perfect.

God is perfect in everything that He does. His love is so huge that it can't even be fathomed by our human minds. He cares so much for His children that He would send His Son Jesus to die so that He could have a relationship with the rest of us. He will never mess up. In fact, He can't mess up. Everything that He will ever do will be for the betterment of Himself and those who love Him. There are times when that doesn't seem true, but it is. That means that it doesn't matter how good your dad on Earth is, he will never measure up to your Father in heaven. And your dad's dad could never measure up to your Father in heaven. Nobody can measure up to your Father in heaven.

You see, God's love for His children is literally perfect. When He looks at us He sees His children, and He has perfect fatherly characteristics. You will never have to worry about God leaving you or your family. You will never have to worry about God not being able to provide. You will never have to worry that God will hurt you physically or emotionally.

I know that there are some dads out there that seem perfect. In fact, they seem a little too perfect. It's almost like they have never messed up in their entire lives. I know of some people who have dads like that and it intimidates them. They constantly live their lives trying to be good enough for their "always perfect" earthly dad. Any time they mess up in even the slightest way, this overwhelming feeling of fear comes over them because they feel as if their dad will disown them because of their mistakes. More often than not, the dad that seems "perfect" because he never messes up can really be prideful, self-centered, unforgiving, not understanding of the concept of grace.

But guess what, our Heavenly Father is overflowing with grace. He sees everything, so there isn't a single mess-up we could ever hide from Him. Fortunately, there isn't a single thing we could ever do to make Him stop loving us. There isn't a single thing he's unwilling to forgive. God's grace abounds forever. It isn't just available for the people who tell small white lies and never really "mess up." It's available for the murderers and the sexually immoral. It's available for the worst sinner and the people who seem to have it all together. God will never toss you out of the family. He will love you through everything and call you His beloved.

FROM FALIURE TO FREEDOM

I've been involved with the ministry of Young Life for several years. I participated in it when I was in high school and now I'm a Young Life leader. If I have noticed anything over the years of being involved in this ministry, it's that people are beginning to feel like failures at younger and younger ages.

I took a group of middle school guys to a Young Life camp in central Florida called Southwind. It's a middle schooler's paradise. It has a huge water slide and an awesome whiffle ball field. The food is some of the best you can have. Not to mention that it has an endless supply of junk food at the snack shop. I love it down there, and I know that my guys do too. It's one of the most fun places on Earth, but it's also a place where major heart change happens.

On this trip one of my guys opened up to the group multiple times. It was as if he had wanted to say this stuff for a very long time, and once he finally got the chance he couldn't stop. The first night he talked for seven minutes straight about how he was the failure of his family. He felt like he always let his parents down when it came to grades and athletics. He mentioned how he felt like his sister hated him, and he called himself fat multiple times. He was talking as if everything that had ever gone wrong in his life was his fault and he thought his parents felt the same way. Over the course of the next few nights he went deeper and deeper with how he felt. He talked more about how he was a failure to his family and about how he was the loser of his friend group. The stuff he was saying broke my heart because he genuinely believed every word of it. This guy was 12 years old and was talking about how much of a disappointment he was to everyone and how he was exhausted because he could never live up to people's expectations.

This 12-year-old kid talked about how fat he was and that no girls would ever like him. I know that I'm biased because he is one of my close friends and my Young Life kid, but believe me when I say that he isn't fat at all. The rest of the guys in my group rallied around him and spoke truth into his life about how he was the only person who viewed himself that way. Absolutely nobody else thought he was fat, but the enemy had wrapped his hands around his thought life and had convinced him of all this stuff. He was convinced he was a failure to his parents. He was convinced he was a loser and fat. He was convinced that no girls would ever like him.

This shows that literally anyone can fall into this trap. He was still just a young kid and was already feeling this way. But everything changed for him on the fourth night of camp. The camp speaker shared the amazing truth that Jesus died for our sins so that we could have an eternal relationship with God. That message struck a chord with my young friend.

After the talk was done we had the opportunity to go outside and be alone with God for a few minutes. We wrote a letter to God and spent time in prayer. When it was time to head back to the cabin I saw my guy standing on the sidewalk with his head down, crying. I walked up to him and immediately could tell what was going on in his heart. We walked over to a grassy field in camp and lay down and looked up at the stars and started talking. He was going on and on about how he feels terrible for letting God down by sinning, and how he will never be able to live up to everyone's expectations for him. All I had to do was lie there next to him and listen. I knew God was working in his heart.

The next fifteen minutes of this story will stay with me for the rest of my life. As we lay there in this grassy field, tears filled the conversation and I could tell that his heart was hurting. I just simply started telling him about the characteristics of Jesus. We talked about how he has the opportunity to be adopted into a family that is beyond any that he has ever known. We talked about what it's like for me since I know that God is my Heavenly Father and how freeing that is. We talked about how he has the opportunity to be completely holy in God's eyes and that at the end of the day that's all that matters. I could see his eyes clear up as he looked at me and said, "Jake, I want that."

So right then and there as we were lying in this field at a Young Life camp in central Florida, my 12-year-old friend went from death to life through Jesus. He was adopted into a divine family and I could see how it changed him. The rest of the week he talked about how awesome Jesus was instead of how he viewed himself as a loser. His whole life changed that week, and now he is experiencing life to the full as a child of God.

THE PRAYER

My prayer is that we ditch the self-proclaiming definitions of ourselves and chase after God's definition of who we are. Let's ignore the instinct of feeling like a failure when we don't succeed in something and instead look at who God says we are in His Word. There is absolutely no failure so big that could ever change the fact that every Christian is a child of God. There is absolutely no expectation that you could fall short of that would make God stop loving you. Like how my dad loved me even when I messed up, God loves His sons and daughters so much more.

I pray that we look past our failures, that we see our new family and the freedom that comes with it, and that we attach "child of God" to our core identity.

| | CH. 8 | |

IMAGES

I was blessed with the opportunity to play football in the AT&T Georgia Junior Bowl when I was in high school. Some of the biggest names in the sport from the state of Georgia were there. I was on a team with Nick Chubb who ended up being a standout running back for the University of Georgia, and I played against Raekwon McMillan who won a national championship playing linebacker for Ohio State. It was one of the greatest experiences in my athletic career, but it wasn't the greatest experience I ever had with that all-star game.

Three years after I played in the Junior Bowl I was asked to come back and speak to the new players. I was extremely excited to see some old friends who helped run the game, but I was even more excited about sharing the Word of God with people who were sitting in the same seats I sat in three years earlier. I started working on my message as soon as I was asked to speak.

I started thinking back to what I would have needed to hear when I was playing in that game. I tried to send myself back in time and remember everything that was going through my head when I was there. I thought about how there were dozens and dozens of reporters there. They would fill up the conference room of the hotel we were staying in and call different players in for interviews and pictures. I also remember the way the players interacted with each other. The 5-stars hung out with the other 5-stars, the 4-stars with 4-stars, and so on. If you weren't one of the top players there, then the media didn't pay you much attention.

I might have been a football standout from my little hometown, but compared to a lot of the guys at that all-star game, I just didn't quite measure up. The director of the game did an amazing job communicating that football isn't everything in life, but that went against everything I had heard growing up in my hometown. So when I saw that I wasn't getting pulled into the conference room for interviews as much as some of the other guys were, it made me mad. Three years later, I relived that moment of anger and the Lord immediately laid on my heart what I should speak about: identity.

The reason I felt the calling to speak on identity was because that's what I struggled with so much when I was playing in the all-star game. I viewed myself as only a football player, and I know that many other kids felt the same way. I remembered how upset I was that the media didn't give me the attention I thought they should have. Those frustrations had led to one of the most treacherous times in my life.

I remember staying up late at night in my hotel room in Atlanta the week of the game wondering why I wasn't getting noticed as much as some of the other guys. I had landed on the conclusion that I was simply too slow. I weighed 245 pounds at the time of the all-star game and I was strong as an ox. But I knew I was nowhere near the fastest kid on the field. That week I became determined to get faster.

The next six months were some of the most dramatic I had ever experienced. I changed my diet and added another workout in the morning before class. I could tell I was getting faster, and the next thing I knew I had lost 55 pounds and was headed into the state semi-finals in soccer. I no longer cared about my speed for football. It was clear that I had become one of the fastest guys on the soccer field, and that was good enough for me. However, I had become addicted to the feeling of working out. It was no longer about performance for me, but appearance. I became obsessed with my diet and my body, and I was always scheming about how I could make myself look better.

I would wake up early during the summer and go work out before my day started. Then before I went to bed I would do 400 pushups to get ready for the next intense day of training. Nothing wrong with that, but I began to think that it was everything in life. I put my body appearance on a pedestal, and working out very quickly became an idol in my life. The worst thing is that I didn't even notice it. I was completely fine in my eyes.

Now allow me to say that there is absolutely nothing wrong with working out and being healthy. I still work out and eat right! I encourage it, actually. However, it can be a very slippery slope when we start to think about it all the time. Being healthy can definitely become an idol in our lives, and that idolatry is only encouraged by all of the pictures we see on social media every single day. The worst part about it is that so many times we see people try to be "healthy" by doing things that are detrimental to their bodies.

Our culture is flooded with people who have eating disorders. Depression is at an all-time high, and people are constantly fed images of what they're supposed to look like through social media outlets. If you believe that those three things are unrelated to each other, then I would like to nicely tell you that you're wrong.

IN HIS OWN IMAGE

The amount of filth we see on social media, the Internet, and television has drastically impacted the way we see ourselves. The number of people I have walked through life with who have suffered from eating disorders is frightening. Some of them are the most confident people you could ever meet. Yet still they get trapped in this false reality of thinking that they have to look a certain way in order to be beautiful. Guys, I don't want you to check out on me here, because I have known my fair share of men who have struggled with the same thing. Just because society has labeled it a female problem doesn't mean that men can't struggle with it.

The most heartbreaking thing about this disordered thinking is that it completely contradicts what we find in Scripture. Nowhere in the Bible does it mention anything about a certain level of beauty we have to obtain. It doesn't say that we have to weigh a certain amount and it definitely doesn't say that we should compare our outward appearance to other people.

Remember, the first and truest description of mankind came from God:

> *So God created man in his own image,*
> *in the image of God he created him;*
> *male and female he created them.*
> (Genesis 1:27, ESV)

In His own Image. You are created in the image of God. The seal that is stamped across your core says, "In the Image of God." At the very center of every human on Earth is the true identity that we all share—images of God.

If that doesn't rock you to your core then I highly encourage you to read it again.

This is something that is said in church all the time, but it very rarely sticks with people. It has become merely simplistic Christian knowledge instead of absolute truth that wrecks our hearts and shows us who we really are.

INDESCRIBABLE BEAUTY

God is absolutely incredible. He is perfect in every way possible. He is matchless in power and we can't even fathom his majesty. He is beautiful. In fact, He is the most beautiful being in all of existence. There is not a single thing in all of creation that comes close to comparing with the beauty of the One who created it all. In Acts 9, Saul (who we know better as Paul) found this out firsthand while he was walking down the road:

> *As he [Saul] neared Damascus on his journey,*
> *suddenly a light from heaven flashed around*

him. He fell to the ground and heard a voice say to him, "Saul, Saul, why do you persecute me?"

"Who are you, Lord?" Saul asked.

"I am Jesus, whom you are persecuting," he replied. . . .

Saul got up from the ground, but when he opened his eyes he could see nothing. So they led him by the hand into Damascus. For three days he was blind, and did not eat or drink anything. (Acts 9:3–5, 8–9, NIV)

The crazy thing about this is that the bright light that came down from heaven was just a glimpse of the indescribable beauty of God Almighty. That one glimpse of the glory of God was enough to blind Paul for three days and change him from the persecutor of Christians to the proclaimer of Jesus.

Another rare firsthand view of the majesty of God's beauty was given to Moses in the Old Testament. Moses was talking with the Lord on Mount Sinai, and the Lord was telling Moses that He would go with him because He was pleased with Moses and knew him by name. Then Moses asked God to show him His glory. God responded like this:

And the LORD said, "I will cause all my goodness to pass in front of you, and I will proclaim

> *my name, the LORD, in your presence. I will*
> *have mercy on whom I will have mercy, and I*
> *will have compassion on whom I will have*
> *compassion. But," he said, "you cannot see my*
> *face, for no one may see me and live."*
>
> *Then the LORD said, "There is a place near me*
> *where you may stand on a rock. When my glo-*
> *ry passes by, I will put you in a cleft in the rock*
> *and cover you with my hand until I have*
> *passed by. Then I will remove my hand and you*
> *will see my back; but my face must not be*
> *seen."*
> (Exodus 33:19–23, NIV)

Just the face of God is something so incredibly wonderful that nobody can see it and remain alive. Moses couldn't handle the full beauty of God. Nobody can. In fact, just seeing the back of God did something spectacular to Moses:

> *When Moses come down from Mount Sinai with*
> *the two tablets of the covenant law in his hands,*
> *he was not aware that his face was radiant be-*
> *cause he had spoken with the LORD. When Aaron*
> *and all the Israelites saw Moses, his face was ra-*
> *diant, and they were afraid to come near him.*
> (Exodus 34:29–30, NIV)

Moses saw the glory of God, and the matchless beauty that comes with it, and his face become radiant. His face was literally glowing. How great God's beauty must be.

The beauty of God is unlike anything we will ever encounter on Earth. It has the power to change our entire lives. Scripture shows us that once someone sees even a glimpse of the beauty of Christ they will never be the same again. Their heart will be shattered into a million microscopic pieces and then it will be put back together in a way that is newer, alive, and more beautiful. The beauty of God is so incredible that our human minds can't even fathom its greatness. Seeing even a glimpse of His beauty causes some kind of physical response. In Paul's case, it left him blind for three days. In Moses' case, it caused his face to glow golden. But no matter what, the beauty of God's glory causes a reaction.

I'm sure that some of you are thinking that nothing like that has ever happened to you before. You're thinking that you've never been blinded and your face has definitely never become radiant. Well, if that's you, then I encourage you to recall the last time you saw the leaves change during autumn in a way that was so incredible it left you speechless. Or how about if you've been to the foothills of a mountain range and the sheer vastness of the horizon brought you to tears. What about the first time you saw a shooting star and all you could think to do was yell and point and jump up and down. Those are all physical reactions that our body generates when we get a glimpse into the beauty of God Almighty.

So, guys, let's try our hardest to wrap our brains around just how beautiful our God is. Now let's try to wrap our brains around the fact that we are each specifically and uniquely made in His image. We are image-bearers of the most beautiful Being in all of existence. We bear the image of the beauty that blinded Paul and caused Moses' face to glow. The God that created the heavens with just a word from His mouth decided that you were going to be made in His likeness. All of the beauty in the known universe combined doesn't compare to the beauty of the One who made you and me, and that is ground to stand on and shout His praise.

KILLING COMPARISON

Part of the reason I struggled so much with my self-image when I was in high school was because of the social media accounts I followed. I saw tons of people who looked flawless on the workout pages I looked at. All I could think about was how I didn't look anything like these people who were supposedly the standard for being physically fit. But then God opened my eyes to see a glimpse of His beauty. That's when I realized that comparison had been dominating my life without me even knowing it. I decided that I wasn't going to let that

We bear the image

of the beauty that

blinded Paul and

caused Moses' face to glow.

happen anymore. I believed in a God who was beautiful in every way, and I knew that I was made in His image. That is when God started killing comparison. Think about it: God is the most beautiful being in existence, and you are made in His image. That means that the image you carry everywhere you go is beautiful. That means that beauty is at the very center of who you are as a person.

I believe in a God who is so incredibly spectacular, He can kill comparison altogether. Once we start living in the truth that we are all made in God's likeness, we will stop worrying about how society says our self-image is supposed to be and we will focus on the God-image that is in each and every one of us. It will no longer matter if you're blonde, brunette, skinny, not skinny, short, tall, or in the middle. All of the superficial, surface-layer garbage that the world feeds us will start to fade to the back, as the miraculous truth of who you really are makes its way to the front. The social media icons that you idolize will no longer seem to be perfect, but instead you will long for them to know Jesus and the truth of who they are.

If you're reading this right now and you are one of those people who have a ton of social media followers, then I pray that you leverage your influence to spread this message through that outlet. Social media is an amazing tool of communicating messages. In one second, millions of people can read something that we put out there. News travels so fast it's scary. However, right now social media is plagued by all the wrong messages of the world.

Imagine if just one person who is famous on Instagram started spreading the message that our identity isn't found in earthly variables, but rather in a heavenly constant. Think of all the life change that could happen for people when they see that the person they look up to isn't promoting the same basic junk everyone else is, but instead they are promoting the gospel and how our identity is rooted in the fact that we are all images of God. More and more people would begin letting go of the pressure they feel to be perfect, and they would realize that it's more about progress than perfection. And not progress when it comes to physical characteristics, but progress when it comes to God-ly character. So if you are one of those people who are prominent on social media, then I highly encourage you to think about the message you are spreading. And if you aren't one of those famous people then I still encourage you to think of the message you are spreading. I encourage you to leverage the influence you have on the 100, 200, or 300 people that follow you. We are all message carriers. The only thing that's different about us is the message we carry.

I know it seems like I have bashed social media pretty hard, but I want to say that I really don't hate it. I have Instagram and Facebook accounts and I use them regularly. I think it's a wonderful way to stay connected, informed, and entertained while you're waiting at the doctor's office. It's also a great way to avoid being awkward in a crowd of people you don't know. Just look at your phone. So it's not the media I object to; it's the messages they tend to spread.

One thing that can be a great habit for all of us when dealing with social media is to ask ourselves how we feel when we close the app. After we exit from Twitter, Instagram, Facebook, or any other social media outlet, we should have a very real conversation with ourselves about whether we feel empowered or deflated. This will show us whether our social media habits are helpful or harmful.

THE PRAYER

This chapter has been an extremely difficult one to write. I have tried to explain the beauty of God, and that is not humanly possible. I've walked on a tightrope trying to explain how I hate the messages that are spread through social media, not social media itself. And I've tried to convey all of this in a way that encourages you to focus on how the beauty of God's image is stamped on your life. All three of those things I have found to be extraordinarily challenging to write about. However, I have also found them to be exceptionally amazing at the same time.

I pray that you all start believing in a God who is big enough to kill comparison in our hearts. The message we carry is so important. It's a prominent way by which the world sees us. I pray that we all start carrying the message of who we really are, and that by doing so we will naturally carry the name of Jesus to people who need Him.

This chapter has wrecked my life, and I pray it does the same for each of you. It's an awesome thing when you're able to put down the everyday pressures that come from today's world and pick up your Scripture. God is in the business of loving you for who you are, not how you look. And who are you? You are an image of the most beautiful being in existence.

| | CH. 9 | |

FREE

My family is one that absolutely loves all things sports. We watch anything from the big NASCAR race to the Division II college football playoffs. It really doesn't matter what sport it is, or even what team it is; we are most likely going to be interested enough to watch it for a few hours.

This phenomenon isn't all that abnormal where I grew up. I'm from a small town in central Georgia, and sports pretty much run the place, especially football. It seems like every man in town has some type of miraculous sports story that has obviously become polluted and exaggerated over the years. Sports were woven into the fabric of my town's culture, and there was no exception when it came to me, my dad, and my brother.

As I've mentioned, I grew up playing soccer and football. I was always much better at soccer, but I loved football more. This was most likely because my dad, in addition to being a principal, was a football coach, and every man in my family had grown up playing it. My brother is four years older than me, so I grew up watching him play both soccer and football, too. As a kid, there were two people in my life that I can truly remember wanting to be like when I was older: my dad and my brother. That meant being the best athlete I could be.

I remember when I was in the seventh grade I had the first real conversation with someone outside of my family about playing sports in college. It was with one of my teachers in the computer lab. He had seen me play both soccer and football and he believed that I had a future in both. So he sat me down one day and talked to me for the entire class period about which one I would choose to play in college if I was forced to pick. I honestly didn't know that day, and I thought about that question every day for a long time. Finally, after about a year and a half of trying to decide which one I would choose, I landed on football. I think it was because my brother was being heavily recruited for college football at the time and decided to commit to play for Coach Mike Gundy at Oklahoma State. The whole town was excited for him and he had several full-page articles written about him in the sports page of the local newspaper. From that day on I knew that I had to play football at the highest collegiate level or else I would be a letdown to my family and my town.

For the next five years I continued to play both football and soccer. I would pour way more time and effort into football, though. I pretty much lived at my high school. I would spend hours in the weight room every day, and then when I finally got home from practice at night I would watch game and practice film. My entire day would be consumed with becoming the best football player I could be so that I would live up to these expectations that I put on myself. It was working, too. I was getting better and better and I knew it. As my junior year came around, I was voted the region's most valuable offensive player in soccer and was asked to play in the all-star football game I talked about earlier, the AT&T Georgia Junior Bowl. The founder of this all-star game was a man named Joe Burns who played in the NFL for the Buffalo Bills for many years and was a hall-of-fame running back at Georgia Tech. My life was going exactly how I felt it was supposed to go.

For the remainder of my junior year I would get called out of at least one class each day to go to the gym and meet with a college football coach. I was receiving letters and visits from schools like the

University of Georgia, Auburn, Florida State, Georgia Tech, and Cincinnati. However, all of the attention I was receiving from them wasn't adding up to anything. I would have visits and letters and phone calls every single day, but nothing more. Not a single school had offered me any type of athletic scholarship yet, and I started freaking out thinking it was never going to happen.

After a crazy junior year filled with losing 55 pounds, a severe knee injury, and a major muscle tear in my back, I was determined to get my first Division I scholarship offer by the end of the summer. I had been invited to several camps throughout the summer, and the first ones on the schedule were Marshall, Princeton, and Yale. These three camps all happened in about a week's time, and my parents made sure they did everything they could to allow me to be at all three. I'm not really sure what happened during that week, but something caused me to start having severe anxiety. I performed extremely well at all three camps, but still did not receive a scholarship offer. I began having these haunting thoughts that everyone in my town was going to view me as a failure if I didn't perform on the same level as my All-American brother.

That's when I realized I didn't work so hard at football because of my passion for the game. I worked so hard at football out of fear. I was scared that I would amount to nothing as an athlete. I was afraid to be considered a failure by my community. I was fearful of becoming someone who "almost made it." That realization made me absolutely resent everything about the game of football. I stopped enjoying practices, I stopped watching extra game and practice film, and I decided to clear my summer schedule and not go to any more college camps. I hated football for what it had done to me and how it had made me feel. I hated the anxiety it brought me and the sleepless nights of wondering about my future. I was trapped and bound up by these chains that were caused by operating my entire life out of fear of not being good enough. I started playing football out of obligation. The only reason I continued to play in my senior year was because I didn't want to let my teammates down. I had no love for the game anymore. I only had fear.

Nonetheless, I ended up sticking with my decision to play football in college after a pretty successful senior year. I was the leading tackler on the team and was voted all-region in two different positions. I was also the state of Georgia's player of the year in soccer, which allowed me to become my school's first all-state soccer player (I told you I was always better at soccer). It seemed like my life was actually playing out the way I had always dreamed, but I was not happy about it.

Let's fast forward to July after my senior year of high school. My foot had been sore all throughout soccer season and had been giving me fits for the previous six or seven months. So finally, about a month before I was going to move into college and start football camp, we decided to go get it checked out by a doctor who specialized in foot injuries. Lo and behold, my foot had been severely broken for the past seven months and I had no idea. I had always been told to play through the pain, but I still don't know how I was able to play through that. I ended up having to go through a pretty serious surgery in order to have a metal bone placed in my foot. I could feel the weight of all of the made-up expectations from the town coming down on my shoulders as the possibility of never being able to play sports again began to sink in.

This is when God showed me the coolest thing. I was up late at night contemplating my entire life and how I was going to be thought of as a failure because I wasn't going to end up playing college football. I was sitting on the couch in my living room and this overwhelming realization came over me: It was okay if I didn't play college football. It seems pretty elementary, but I had never even considered it before that night. It was like God just opened my eyes to see that football would one day come to an end anyway. If I only defined myself as an athlete, then after four years when my college career was over I would be left wondering who the heck I was. That night was when I realized that God had been showing me that I was called to ministry, not athletics.

There is no real word to describe the way I felt when I walked out of the coach's office one last time after letting him know that I would not be playing football for his school because I felt called into ministry. It was a mixture of terror and obedience. I was terrified about what my future might look like in ministry because it was an avenue that I had never considered. But I also felt calmly obedient because I knew that I was answering God's call on my life. After a few weeks of discerning what steps to take from there, I realized exactly how I felt—free.

It was like I was a new person. I no longer felt trapped by the expectations that I had put on myself. It turns out there wasn't even a single person in my hometown who thought of me as a failure and the entire time it was the enemy feeding me lies and me believing them.

All too often we are horrified of what other people think of us. We may fear how people view our physical selves, whether they think we are annoying, or in my case, whether we are going to fall short of their expectations. This is such an easy fear to have because we all want to fit in and be loved. I think it is probably one of the biggest fears that people of any age have. But I also believe it can be eradicated. If we fully take what Jesus has to offer, and realize that we are in fact sons and daughters of the King of the universe, heirs to His Kingdom alongside Jesus, and images of the most beautiful being in existence, then we will come to walk freely in truth instead of timidly in fear.

FROM DEATH TO LIFE, FROM LIFE TO FREEDOM

I know for a fact that God wants us to live free. He doesn't want us to be bound up by some earthly circumstance that doesn't matter in the grand scheme of things. He wants us to walk in truth and in life. Perhaps one of the most amazing and well-known passages in Scripture shows us this perfectly. It's one of the most-taught stories in all of the Bible, but I want to focus on something that often gets skipped over. The story comes out of John 11 and it's about a man named Lazarus.

Lazarus was the brother of Martha and Mary, and they were from the town of Bethany. Mary was the same woman who lay at Jesus' feet and poured insanely expensive perfume on them and wiped them with her hair. A few months before that, Lazarus had gotten sick while Jesus and His disciples were miles away. So Mary and Martha sent a messenger to Jesus to tell him about Lazarus' condition. Jesus loved Lazarus and the two sisters, but He stayed where He was for two days. He also told all of the disciples about how Lazarus was sick, but that this illness would not end in death. However, after the two days, He said to His disciples that they should travel back to Judea. This seemed like a crazy thing for Jesus to say because the Jews in Judea had just tried to stone Him.

Jesus informed His disciples that Lazarus had "fallen asleep," and that He had to go wake him. His disciples didn't understand what was going on and they told Jesus that if he was asleep it meant that he was resting and should remain that way in order to get better. So then Jesus just came out and told them that Lazarus had died. I'm sure they were all confused because of how Jesus said earlier that the sickness would not end in death. But nevertheless, they went back to Judea and Jesus comforted and wept with Mary and Martha. This is when the story gets insane:

> *Jesus, once more deeply moved, came to the tomb. It was a cave with a stone laid across the entrance. "Take away the stone," he said.*

> *"But, Lord," said Martha, the sister of the dead man, "by this time there is a bad odor, for he has been there four days."*

> *Then Jesus said, "Did I not tell you that if you believe, you will see the glory of God?"*

So they took away the stone. Then Jesus looked up and said, "Father, I thank you that you have heard me. I knew that you always hear me, but I said this for the benefit of the people standing here, that they may believe that you sent me."

When he had said this, Jesus called in a loud voice, "Lazarus, come out!" The dead man came out, his hands and feet wrapped with strips of linen, and a cloth around his face.

Jesus said to them, "Take off the grave clothes and let him go."
(John 11:38–44, NIV)

Come on. Jesus literally told a man that had been dead four days to get up AND HE DID! That's so incredible. I think we have become numb to the fact that this isn't just some story in a really old book, but instead it actually happened. There really was a man named Lazarus who was from Bethany. He really did have sisters named Martha and Mary, and he really did die for four days until Jesus really did bring him back to life. That is absolutely amazing and I think that every time that story is taught in church there should be screams in the congregation and people yelling "Amen" as loud as they can.

Jesus brings people from death to life. He did it to Lazarus and He still does it now. He brings people who are spiritually dead into being fully alive through Him. But the coolest thing that we can learn from this passage is something that I believe is so overlooked. After Jesus brought Lazarus from death to life He didn't just leave. He didn't say, "Okay, my work here is done. You're welcome, Laz." No, He said something else. When Lazarus walked out of that tomb alive Jesus said, "Take off the grave clothes and let him go."

In Jesus' time, when someone passed away, they wrapped their hands and feet together with linen. They also wrapped their faces with it. It was a traditional "dressing" for a dead person. So when Lazarus walked out of the tomb alive, he was still dressed as a dead person. His hands were still bound with linen and his face was covered up by cloth. Clearly that was not okay with Jesus. He just brought him from death to life. He wanted him living freely because of that, not bound up in the same clothes he was wearing when he was dead.

I think that we can all learn something exceptional from this. Going from death to life through Jesus is the most pivotal, important, extraordinary, and beautiful thing that can ever happen to us. But Jesus doesn't want us to be alive in Him while living with the same shackles that bound us in death. Obviously He loves when we are saved, but I believe that He looks at every one of us in that moment when He first brings us from death to life and He says, "Take off the grave clothes."

Jesus' calling on our lives after we enter into His family is not a calling of bondage. So many people view Christianity as a set of rules that hold them back instead of a miraculous series of events that set them free. Jesus' death on the cross was not meant to enclose Christians inside of a room while being shackled by a list of rules. Jesus' resurrection from the grave broke those shackles and opened the door to that room so that we could live a life of abundant freedom.

For myself, I can look back and say confidently that I lived a good chunk of my Christian life with the grave clothes still on. I would operate out of fear, not even realizing that there was any other way to live. But thankfully, through coming from death to life in Jesus, there is another way. We can be free. We can feel free. We can live free.

WE AREN'T CALLED
TO LIVE ANXIOUSLY

People today are experiencing more anxiety than ever. This anxiousness comes from their work, from their fear of not being accepted, and especially from the way others view them. In my case, I was anxious because of the fear that people would view me as a failure. It's an easy trap to fall into because the world tells us that we should have everything figured out by the time we are 18. Satan uses that pressure and tees off on so many of our

But thankfully, through

coming from death to life

in Jesus,

there is another way.

We can be free.

We can feel free.

We can live free.

thought lives by saying that we are failures, less than, not loved, or simply not good enough.

That is the complete opposite of the gospel. The literal heart behind the gospel is the fact that God loved us so much He sent His Son to die on a cross in our place. The most famous Bible verse of all time shows us that (John 3:16). Even though most of us know that verse, we so often look past God's love and only see fear that is coming from non-gospel sources.

Jesus gives us something to hold onto in Luke chapter 12:

> *And he said to his disciples, "Therefore I tell you, do not be anxious about your life, what you will eat, nor about your body, what you will put on. For life is more than food, and the body more than clothing. Consider the ravens: they neither sow nor reap, they have neither storehouse nor barn, and yet God feeds them. Of how much more value are you than the birds! And which of you by being anxious can add a single hour to his span of life? If you are not able to do as small a thing as that, why are you anxious about the rest?"* (Luke 12:22–26, ESV)

Jesus doesn't call us to live in fear of the future, but He calls us to live in freedom during the present. This passage is warning us of the anxiety that the world can throw at us, and it's telling us to not worry about it! Jesus is saying not to worry about having everything in your life planned out because you can't even add a single hour to your lifespan by doing so. And if you can't even do that, then why worry about anything else?

What good does it do for us to worry about what job we are going to have after we graduate college? Will worrying about it give us our dream job? Of course not. The ravens don't work for anything, yet God still feeds them. How much more valuable are you than the birds? Now Jesus is not saying that we should avoid work and neglect to support ourselves. But what He is saying is that we should seek the Kingdom of God first, not our dream job or our perfect plan for the future.

When we seek the Kingdom first, God shows us that there is nothing in this world to be anxious about. He provides for us. He wants to show us that living completely dependent on Him is more rewarding than doing everything by ourselves. When we work our jobs, we need to work them as well as we possibly can for the glory of God. He will provide us with what we need. When we are in school we need to be the best students we can possibly be, but while seeking the Kingdom first. In doing this He will show you that anxious living is not from Him, and then He will free you of those chains.

O TRAMPLED DEATH, WHERE IS YOUR STING?

A lot of people in this world live in fear of death. They feel as if the uncertainty of the afterlife is too much to handle. I've had conversations with people who don't believe in Jesus and are horrified of death. Not because they think they might go to hell; most of them don't even believe in hell. But they are afraid of just not existing. They are afraid of the darkness that they feel might close around them forever.

I've also talked to Christians who are afraid of death. The thought of eternity scares them. I've heard one person say that forever in heaven is frightening because forever is a long time. Jesus doesn't want this for us. He wants us to look at death the same way He did. He stared the cross down and willingly experienced death because He knew that His story would not end there. He wants us to look death in the eye and know that because of Him we are going to live forever in the greatest place imaginable. And for those of you who think forever is a long time, I encourage you to keep in mind that "time" doesn't exist in heaven. What is 1,000 years on Earth will seem like one day in heaven. We will be so captivated by the radiant beauty of Jesus that nothing else will matter.

When Jesus brings us from death to life He wants our fear of death to go away. He wants us to understand that He defeated death once and for all. He didn't die so that we would be saved by grace through faith in Him but still remain chained up by the fear of death. He died so that we would never experience death and live in complete freedom through Him.

THE PRAYER

There is a specific reason I put this chapter toward the end of the book. I want you to be able to read the previous chapters and let all of the truth of who you really are sink in. I want you to begin to see yourself as a beautiful creation. I want you to know that you are a child of God and that you are alive through Jesus. I want you to understand that you are an image of the most beautiful being in all of existence, and that your identity comes from a heavenly constant instead of an earthly variable. I want you to see yourself as completely blameless because of Jesus' holiness.

I pray that you will walk away from this chapter in complete freedom. Being free isn't just a way to live our lives; it's literally who we are after coming from death to life in Jesus. We are free from fear, we are free from anxiety, and we are free from the sting of death. I pray that you see that as who you truly are.

| | EPILOGUE | |

SAV'S STORY

This is my friend Sav's true story.
I am grateful to her for allowing me to share it with
you, and I pray it touches your heart like it did mine.

The garage door creaked open. Four tiny heads, including my own, turned towards each other with anxious anticipation. We all knew what that sound meant. Quickly, we jumped to our feet and scurried through the kitchen into the garage to greet the man we knew would be getting out of his car any second. This man was our hero. He was our provider. He was our father. This very beautiful exchange of hugs and kisses was a normal daily routine around our little house. My three older sisters and I could not get enough of this man.

While a mother tends to carry with her the "heart" of the home, the father usually assumes the position of protector, provider, and comforter. It was in those moments when my daddy would sweep me up into his arms and hold me tight when I felt the most loved by him. I would also feel it when we would have dance parties in the living room where the music would be louder than the neighbors appreciated, I'm sure. Honestly, I felt it all the time when I was a little kid.

Those moments consumed my childhood and I have never been more grateful for them than I am now. You see, I wish I could just pause my story here to tell you that for the rest of my wonderful, perfect life I was greeted with countless hugs and dances from my father. However, that is not how this story turns out.

But for many years, the happy moments continued. We had daddy-daughter breakfast dates, family yard workdays, tickle fights, and grocery store runs. One particular family yard workday stands out more than the others. My family was attempting to obliterate the massively overgrown bushes in our front yard. My dad had come down with pneumonia a few days prior and was feeling a little under the weather, but he worked hard as my sisters, my mom, and I brought branches and pieces of bush for him to throw into a chipper. The day was long and strenuous, so it only seemed natural for my father to wearily climb up to the bedroom and steal a quick nap before dinner.

I never could have suspected what that nap would be the beginning of. My dad had never been much of a napper. Instead, he tended to be the life of the party. He would wake up at five a.m. every day and have the stamina to last until eleven at night. So we were all more than a little concerned when he began to need a nap every afternoon. Soon he was experiencing vertigo so bad that he needed to wear an eye patch everywhere he went and eventually had to give up driving. His balance was so poor that he frequently fell, and he developed incredible nerve pain and intense headaches. His nerve pain continued to persist until the nerve damage settled in his legs and he was no longer capable of walking or standing without assistance.

Despite the obviousness of my dad's problems, none of us knew how to help him. Dad ran to every doctor, prescription, and "healing service" that he could. After countless doctor visits and various medicines, my dad finally arrived at a doctor that prescribed him steroids.

At the time I had no idea that steroids could cause serious psychological side effects, so I didn't expect the frustration, anxiety, and anger that began to surface in my dad. I would come home night after night to hear my parents arguing loudly, and we kids were shocked. The arguing turned into screaming, and eventually my sisters and I had to intervene before the fighting escalated even more. This sort of evening, one filled with yelling and my dad screaming unrepeatable names at my mom, became a nightly ordeal.

As a 14-year-old girl just entering the world of high school, I had no way of knowing how to handle or process what was happening, and things continued to get worse. My dad went from screaming at my mother to screaming at everyone in the family. He would get so mad that he started hobbling out of the house shouting, "I will never come back! I'm divorcing you!" (colorful language omitted).

Because he was disabled and unable to walk without a walker, my dad continued to come back home within a couple of days of each fight to ensure that he would have a shower and a few good meals. Once those needs were met, he would repeat this cycle and head back out in an angry fit. There were a few nights in particular that stand out more than the others, but I will spare the details. Let's just say that my dad became extremely emotionally abusive. And in some cases even physically abusive.

People could tell me all they wanted that my dad was acting the way he was because of the steroids, or because he was going through something very traumatic. But as a young teenager, I had no interest in giving him the benefit of the doubt. I was in survival mode. We all were. I was so focused on protecting my mom, my sisters, and myself that I didn't have the time or energy to protect him as well. I viewed him as the enemy. I hated my dad. I told my mom to divorce him. I never wanted to see him ever again, much less talk to him. So I made up my mind that I wasn't going to talk to him anymore. For two years I lived in the same house with my dad without speaking a word to him. My dad continued to take the steroids, and he became more and more aggressive and angry.

I had gone from a home full of encouragement and love to a hell filled with lies and hate. When a young girl is told some of the horrible things I was told during this time, she's going to believe at least some of them. Especially if what she's being told is coming from her dad—the man she has looked up to since she was born. I began to believe that I was worthless, unloved, and never enough. Believing my father's abuse completely alienated me from him, but worse, it turned me away from who I really was. I spent years trying to fix what wasn't even broken in me. The enemy had a field day on my thought life, and he hardened my heart like I never thought possible.

The cycle of abuse and abandonment that had begun to dominate my life felt like it would never end. But eventually my dad was taken off the steroids, and about a year later he finally began to come around. The problem now was that he had done so much damage that it was almost unbearable to hear him say he was sorry. I was unwilling to forgive him. I had begun to hate not just my dad, but myself too. I hated how I had responded to him while he was going through the worst time in his life. I hated the things I said to him. I hated the things I said about him. I hated looking at him and hearing his voice. I hated the fact that I believed what he said about me. I hated hearing that I needed to forgive him, and I hated who I had become: a bitter, unforgiving little girl.

Although my dad was back, I felt like I didn't deserve him, that I wasn't worth his time or energy. I began to believe that I wasn't worth anyone's time, energy, or love. My self-image was completely obliterated. This self-doubt poured over into my relationships with other men, as well as with my sweet, sweet Jesus.

For years, my self-loathing devoured any good in my life and lead to depression and insecurity. I ran towards a lifestyle of constantly comparing myself with others—always negatively. I began to feel that if only I changed certain things about myself, then I would be loved and accepted more. If only I could date the "perfect guy," someone who would build me up and tell me I was pretty, then all of my issues from my dad would be reversed.

As I continued in this way of living, I subconsciously decided to make choices based upon the immediate instead of the future.

Fast-forward a year or so and I met this guy I worked with . . . I'll call him Jordan. I thought he was extremely attractive and that he had a pretty funny sense of humor. He was also in an extremely rough season of life. He had just broken up with a girlfriend, and he had recently been arrested. The more we talked the more I felt the Holy Spirit telling me that he was bad news. I didn't care, though. I thought he was so cute. It didn't matter that he was breaking the law or that he was not pursuing a relationship with the Lord. He was showing me the affection and attention I wanted, and I loved it. I loved it when he would hold my hand, or kiss me, or tell me I was beautiful. I needed it. I couldn't live without it. I began to feed on the attention Jordan would give me and I didn't care about all the other times that he would treat me unfairly. My all-consuming thought was Jordan.

We had been dating no longer than two months when he began to push physical boundaries beyond my level of comfort. By this point I had already given up on the idea of trying to connect with him on a spiritual or emotional level. After all, he wasn't following the Lord, and he definitely wasn't willing to talk about emotional issues. But I longed for some sort of connection. I wanted to continue to feel worthy, loved, accepted, and cared for. So I decided that the only way to ensure this happened was to break my physical boundaries. Giving into our passionate lust just about killed me, but we didn't stop. I hated myself for what was going on. But at this point Jordan was the only man in my life telling me what I wanted to hear. He was the only reason my self-esteem had not fallen into a dark abyss. Little did I know, a perfect storm was brewing that ended up hurting my self-image more than I thought possible.

I began to blame myself for every problem in my relationship with Jordan. I felt that it was my fault that we would go too far sexually or that he would treat me unfairly. I even began thinking that it was my fault that my dad hurt me in the first place. All of these lies rained blow after blow on my self-image. I had officially entered into the darkest time in my life and was consumed with depression, anxiety, and the feeling that I would never be good enough.

Eventually I had had enough. I broke up with Jordan. It was not an easy decision at the time, but Jesus began to reveal to me how toxic the relationship had been and how depressed I had become. Jordan had been involved in more illegal activity and had lied to my face about it, and I realized that our year together was the most draining, life-sucking relationship I had ever been in. I regretted ever dating him in the first place.

The way that my relationship with Jordan ended, and the relationship as a whole, taught me so much about myself. I realized how much of my identity I had put into someone calling me beautiful or holding me while he whispered that everything was going to be all right. I also realized how much I tended to put my hope in other people. At one point I had put all of my hope in my dad. He was my everything: my hero, my idol, my superman. I put my security and hope in him because he loved me so well. However, the minute he let me down, I was crushed. I did the same with Jordan. I put my hope in him. And I ended up, once again, devastated.

The truth is that I had become insecure because of how caught up I was in what people thought of me. I was so consumed with what people had to say about me that I had stopped caring what God had to say about me. Growing up, I had always heard that we were supposed to find our identity in Christ, but to be honest, I always thought that was a little cheesy. I didn't even understand what that meant, and I definitely didn't think it would solve my problems. I never saw anything wrong with putting my worth in guys. I mean after all, that's what all the fairy tales taught me. It wasn't until I ended up feeling completely worthless that I realized something was wrong. It was in the moments that my unstable foundation was rocked when I realized there must be a better solution than what I was trying. I began realizing how flawed I was, and how every other human is as well. Once the Lord revealed this to me, I found that no person, place, or thing can take the place only He can fill in my life. Any human I tried to squeeze into that position would crumble under the weight of all that it required. Any thing you rely on to satisfy your need to be accepted will only cause more harm than good in your life. Those temporary placeholders will only leave us with the feeling of rejection and emptiness.

As I sat on my bedroom floor one evening, Jesus began to soften my heart towards my father and towards the idea of forgiving him. This wasn't some insane moment where I saw an angel come down from heaven and strike lightning. This was a very powerful, yet simple occurrence. I felt the Lord speaking to me with the simple question, "If I, the Creator of the universe—the only perfect man to walk the planet—the One who died on the cross on your behalf—the One who healed the sick and walked on water—if I have already forgiven your father, then what right do you have to not forgive him? Are you saying you have more authority than Me?" I sat there on my shaggy carpet baffled at that thought. I forgave my dad in that one moment. But

I was also convicted of the fact that forgiveness is not a onetime event. It is a moment's decision, yes. But it is also a commitment to live in an attitude of constant forgiveness towards that person each and every day.

Haters are going to say, "She's just got daddy issues," and honestly . . . they're not all wrong. I think the reason that so many people are so wounded by their fathers is because fathers and their children have an incredibly special bond. This bond is so unique. It is broken a lot of times because fathers, just like everyone else, are sinful. I think we desire an incredible relationship with our earthly father, and that because the father-child relationship is a reflection of the most amazing relationship in all of history: the intimate, unique, and wonderful relationship we are invited into with our Creator and heavenly Father.

I have been through many seasons that were plagued by comparison, anxiety, depression, and little to no self-esteem. I have idolized pride and people. I have found my security in the things of this world. But I have also realized that this world is full of opinions. And opinions, like anything else, are subject to change. Even so, we are easily influenced by them. Whether we admit it or not, what people say matters. What you say matters.

It has been said, "Comparison is the thief of joy." The real truth is that when I was searching for security in my father, friends, and words that people said to me, I was actually feeding the self-image problems I was trying to escape from. The more I became obsessed with my happiness, the more unhappy I became. I always wondered why that was. The fact is that we were not designed to think about ourselves all the time. We were created to love others. First Corinthians 13:13 (NIV) says:

> And now these three remain: faith, hope and love. But the greatest of these is love.

We are called to love others. When we love others we find joy there. It is a different kind of joy, though. It's one that isn't temporary, but lasts forever. When we love we are truly finding our security in Jesus: "Whoever does not love does not know God, because God is love." (1 John 4:8, NIV)

When we begin spending our time loving others and being like Jesus to those around us, then we will naturally begin to find security in Him. The things we tend to compare ourselves to begin to take the back burner. What my experiences have taught me is that we are brought to life when we focus on the things Jesus says about us instead of what the world says about us. I choose to find my identity and security in Jesus rather than the fleeting things of this world that will never satisfy. Nothing has helped my self-image problem more than uprooting the identity issue that was feeding it.

I can look back at my life a few years ago when I was dating Jordan and see how far I've come. I used to long to be accepted and complimented by him. Now I know how accepted I am by Jesus, and how He loves me more than I could ever imagine. The amount of freedom that I have experienced because of this is supernatural. It's freedom that could only come from a heavenly Father. There is no way I should be healed from all of the hurtful things my father said to me, but I am. There is no way I should feel loved, blameless, or free after the things I did with Jordan, but I do. My perception shifted from worldly to Godly, and so did my view of myself. Jesus showed me that the earthly variables that are present in my life are not the center of my life. I know exactly who I am now, and it's not because some guy is telling me. It's because my God has told me.

| | | |

THE LAST WORD

One of my favorite things about Sav's story is that it shows how people can come out of the darkest times in their lives into some of the most freeing times of their lives. That's the gospel.

I know that there are so many people who will relate to Sav's story on such a personal level. The number of people I know who have been crippled by words spoken over them is insane. They're told that they are unworthy, ugly, not good enough, incapable of being loved. Sometimes by the people they look up to the most. The enemy loves to use these lies against us so that we will fall into the same dark hole Sav was in. Then, when we are in that hole, he attempts to bury us under the weight of unmet expectations.

But it's all a lie. It doesn't matter how many times someone tells you that you're not good enough to be loved, because at the end of the day it will still be a lie. We have truth on our side. It is a historical fact that Jesus was crucified. Willingly He gave His life with you in mind. He didn't fight the cross. He didn't run and try to hide when it was time for Him to be prosecuted. And He didn't lie when Pilate asked Him if He was king of the Jews. Instead He pictured your face, and He pictured my face, and He took those nails in His hands and feet because of His great love for us.

Satan knows that this is true, so he does everything in his power to try to make us not believe it. He wants us to believe that we are so unworthy that not even God can love us. However, Jesus showed us that the best way to counter the lies from the enemy is with absolute truth from God. One of my favorite things to read when I feel unworthy is Psalm 8:

O LORD, our Lord,
how majestic is your name in all the earth!
You have set your glory above the heavens.
Out of the mouth of babies and infants,
you have established strength because of your
*   foes,*
to still the enemy and the avenger.
When I look at your heavens, the work of your
*   fingers,*
the moon and stars, which you have set in
*   place,*
what is man that you are mindful of him,
and the son of man that you care for him?
Yet you have made him a little lower than the
*   heavenly beings*
and crowned him with glory and honor.
You have given him dominion over the works of
*   your hands;*
you have put all things under his feet,
all sheep and oxen,
and also the beasts of the field,
the birds of the heavens, and the fish of the sea,
whatever passes along the paths of the seas.
O LORD, our lord,
how majestic is your name in all the earth!
(Psalm 8, ESV)

My biggest hope for this book is that you understand just how loved you are. The same God who created the heavens, the moon, and the stars cares about you more than you could ever know. He has made you to have dominion over the Earth and take care of His creation. That responsibility alone is enough to know just how much God loves us. He appointed us to take care of His Earth. The planet that is saturated with His glory is our home, and we are its caretakers. I pray that we all start living in a way that reflects this truth.

My prayer is that Sav's words stick with you in your heart. I pray that you take her story and view it as a testament to the faithfulness of God, and I pray that it changes your life. I hope that after reading Sav's story you understand that we really can fight this self-image epidemic that is crippling us all. Our God is big enough to kill comparison altogether. Sav's life is just one example of living, breathing proof that this is true.

Keep your eyes on Jesus.

Keep fighting.

You're incredible.

You're worthy of love.

You're a child of God.

You're Free.

You're made in the image of the most beautiful being in existence.

|| ACKNOWLEDGMENTS ||

Creating this resource was perhaps one of the most challenging yet fun adventures of my life. I have received continuous support throughout the entire journey, and more people than I can write about have helped me along the way.

First I want to thank my beautiful wife, Madeline. You have encouraged me, prayed for me, and you took this dream of mine and made it your own. For that I am forever grateful. I love you.

Kevin Marks and Leighton Ching—y'all have been warriors in this process for me. Your experience in life and work have made this resource what it is, and I could not have done any of it without you guys. Caleb Stanley—Thank you for being a dreamer alongside me. Your prayers and intentional efforts to make this resource known have been incredible.

Savannah Lubben, Lucas Bauer, Zach Katz, and Emilie Johnson—You four were a part of the very beginning of this journey. Each of you spent countless hours huddled in my old apartment dreaming and praying about what this could be. I am forever indebted to y'all. To my mom and dad—I have never received such support as I have from you two. You have cheered me on my entire life, but your roles in this process are ones I will cherish forever. Slate Fluker—Thank you for being a dreamer. You believed in me when even I thought I was crazy for trying to create this resource.

Joe Burns—Thank you for giving me a voice, and for believing in this vision. Your generosity and faith has made this resource what it is. Courtney Gross—you have been so influential in the construction of *Image.* Your feedback has proven to be so important to this process.